DISCUSSION GROUP LEADERS GUIDE

SUPPLEMENT TO THE WHITE ALLY TOOLKIT WORKBOOK

Viveca, we love your commitment to racial equity!

David Campt
6-21-19

BY DAVID W. CAMPT, PHD

I AM Publications

Discussion Group Leaders Guide: Supplement to the White Ally Toolkit Workbook

I AM Publications

(617) 564-1060

contact@iampubs.com

www.iampubs.com

Printed in the United States of America

First Edition, 2018

ISBN: 978-1-943382-05-7

ACKNOWLEDGEMENTS

To Chad B. and Sue P. in Portland OR, and Kelly M. and Stephen B. in Richmond VA – your enthusiasm to form learning communities provided invaluable pressure;

To the Sirloin House and especially Santana's in Eden NC, for graciously allowing extended stays from very modest orders;

To Lisa, for the pushes that come with your being a role model of living one's best life;

To McCrae and Dayne, who always have believed deeply in this project and who have reminded me of the need to bear down and create;

To Deborah and Larry, who have had to extend more patience and accommodation than coaches should have to;

To Ivan, whose constant enthusiasm for and ever growing understanding of the project fuels my confidence that platforms that teach compassion are possible;

To Ngozi, for doing the right amount stepping on the gas and stomping on the brakes;

To Vietta and Arnai, for teaching me that you must to stick with it, even when others join you in quietly questioning whether success will end the story;

To James and Geraldine, whose increasingly boiled-down essence reminds me that great dialogue sometimes has great words and sometimes has great silences;

To all allies in the struggle to free humanity from needless divisions.

TABLE OF CONTENTS

INTRODUCTION

This Discussion Group Leaders Guide is designed to serve as a supplement to the White Ally Toolkit Workbook. The Workbook includes reflection questions, exercises, commentary, and other material that can help anti-racism allies[1]—especially those who are white but others as well—become more influential during encounters with people who are skeptical that racism against people of color is a problem still needing specific attention[2]. The Workbook was written as a compendium of resources aimed at helping individual allies on their journey to greater effectiveness.

This Guide is designed to help a learning community of allies navigate through the Workbook in an optimal sequence. This Guide is designed to be used by discussion leaders and facilitators in a sequence of four to five sessions that will help a group of allies (three to ten people is the suggested group size) make progress in trying to integrate empathy-based approaches into their daily anti-racism practice.

This First Edition of the Guide provides group leaders with very detailed instructions about progressing through the four sessions that comprise Course #1: Ally Fundamentals. The Guide also provides general instructions on navigating through the rest of the Workbook, which can be completed in two additional courses.

---

1   In this project, people who believe racism against people of color is more significant than racism against whites are called anti-racism allies, or just allies.
2   These people are referred to as racism skeptics.

INTRODUCTION

The table below shows the suggested path through the Workbook.

	Name	Duration	Key Topics
Course #1	Ally Fundamentals	4 sessions	Unconscious Bias White Privilege
Course #2	Hot Topics	5 sessions	Race and Economics Race and the Law
Course #3	Healing History	6 sessions	Immigration No racists anymore Athletes and Protests Racism was long ago

COURSES THAT CAN HAVE MULTIPLE DURATIONS OF COMMITMENT

The Ally Fundamentals Course is based on four sessions, each lasting two to three hours. The sessions should take place no more than once per week and no less frequently than once per six weeks. Having a reasonable amount of time between sessions allows participants to test what they learn "in the wild," meaning during interactions with family, friends, acquaintances, and strangers. Here is how long it will take a group to progress through the entire series of courses at various meeting frequencies.

	Course #1	Course #1 & #2	Courses #1, #2 & #3
Once per week	One month	9 weeks (2 months)	15 weeks (one semester)
Once per 2 weeks	Two months	20 weeks (5 months)	30 weeks (about ½ year)
Once per month	4 months (1 semester)	9 months – 1 academic year	15 months

This Guide is not designed to create dialogue between skeptics and allies. This course is intended for anti-racism allies, which this project defines as, primarily, the 45% of white people who think that racism against people of color is a bigger problem than so-called racism against white people. The other 55% of white people who think that racism against whites is just as important as a social problem as racism against people of color are called "racism skeptics." To date, the ACT project has been focused on giving allies both encouragement and the skills to be more persuasive in the context of one-on-one and small-group dialogue with racism skeptics. At this time, this guide is NOT designed for the purpose of creating ally-to-skeptic dialogue within the sessions.

NO REQUIREMENTS THAT PARTICIPANTS HAVE TAKEN THE WORKSHOP

One of the primary ways that ACT helps allies is by providing workshops that happen in communities or online. Many people who have bought the Workbook or this Guide learned about it through these workshops. This Ally Fundamentals course has been purposely designed to be useful whether participants have attended an introductory workshop or not.

This is achieved by including an optional component designed to orient participants to the approaches and key methods of the project. This component is called the Getting Grounded Segment and it lasts between sixty to ninety minutes. (Think of the Getting Grounded Segment as Session 0. Group leaders will need to decide whether doing the Getting Grounded Segment is necessary. If the leader(s) choose to conduct the getting Grounded Segment, they also will have to decide whether to make this an additional Session or to integrate this component within Session 1.

EACH PARTICIPANT SHOULD HAVE THE WORKBOOK

This guide is intended to be used in the context of a group in which every member has a PDF or hardcopy version of the White Ally Toolkit Workbook. Participants should plan on bringing to the session meeting either their entire Workbook or the relevant p.s.

GROUP LEADERS DO NOT NEED TO BE EXPERIENCED FACILITATORS

It is not required that the leader(s) of the session be experienced in facilitation. Rather, they only need to have the ability to provide basic leadership to a group. This Guide has been written so that inexperienced facilitators can follow the step-by-step instructions and create an engaging experience for the group. Each session and segment within it also includes learning objectives, so that experienced facilitators can ignore the more detailed instructions and implement whatever steps they want in service of those objectives. Leaders can follow the step-by-step instructions but it is best if they review everything in advance.

INTRODUCTION

Ideally, a group leader will invest twenty to forty minutes before the meeting in reviewing this Guide and preparing their own answers to some questions that will be posed to the group. If the group has a number of people who are comfortable leading groups, it would not be unreasonable to give multiple people the chance to lead a session during the course.

THE GUIDE CAN BE CUSTOMIZED FOR SPECIFIC SUBPOPULATIONS

The Guide provides the group leader with some options for customizing the course to particular populations, professions, or communities. It does this by providing population-specific segments for each session—near the beginning (Optional Segment 1.5) and near the end (Optional Segment 4.5). Leaders might use these segments to reinforce the idea that the group's work on their allyship is also aligned with their sense of shared identity.

Quotation highlighting an important value for the session (Segment 1.5)—These quotations are designed as a focal point that might solidify the sense of common purpose within the group. The quotations emphasize an important value that is related to the session content and that anti-racism allies always need to keep in mind.

Excerpt from a Respected Source (Segment 1.5)—These excerpts have been chosen because they relate to the important value in the session and because they are from a source that enjoys wide respect in the community.

Inspiring Role Model (Segment 4.5)—These short summaries provide a concrete example of someone who has done notable ally work and who, broadly speaking, shares a common connection with the participants. This segment helps participants learn about and be encouraged by someone who decided—perhaps while still demonstrating some flaws as an ally—to take a risk in service of their commitment to fight oppression.

The community-building material has been constructed based on the idea that there is an overarching value that applies to each session:
- **Session 1:** Recommitting to the Ally Journey. Potential Value: Commitment

- **Session 2:** Unconscious Bias. Potential Value: Humility and Reflection
- **Session 3:** Unearned Racial Advantage (White Privilege). Potential Value: Unfairness
- **Session 4:** Sustaining the Ally Journey. Potential Value: Persistence

This First Edition of the Guide includes community-specific material for three groups: 1) specialists in conflict resolution and the facilitation arts, 2) professionals in social work, counseling, public health, addiction treatment and related fields, and 3) people of faith who would consider themselves conservative Christians. The quotations, excerpts, and role model descriptions are provided in appendices at the back of the guide. Some suggestions about what a group leader might say to introduce the material is provided in the appendices as well. The main body of the Guide has placeholder indicators that show where this material might be used in the course of a session. Additional appendices of supplemental material for other specific populations will be distributed on the ACT website as they become available.

ROLE OF SUPPLEMENTARY VIDEO CONTENT
There is supplemental video content available that group leaders have the option of using if they think it will enhance the group's learning experience.

Some of this video content is available at no cost on ACT's YouTube p. and the free part of the ACT website. There is also professionally edited and curated content available within the subscriber section of our website (www.allyconversationtoolkit.com), which can be used to enhance group learning. Group leaders will need to decide whether to use the video content at all, and if so, what content they will suggest participants watch at home and what will be shown during the meeting.

SOME GENERAL GROUND RULES FOR GROUP LEADERS
- Feedback sessions—always lead with the positives, and if possible, try to end with positive statements as well.
- Be ready to provide an example of key points that you want to convey.

INTRODUCTION

- If you want to rely on video, call up the site before the meeting so you don't create unnecessary delays.

- Plan how to prioritize sections so that you make sure you get to the key content.

- Depending on the culture of the group, it may be helpful to explicitly ask for extra time in cases when the processes run long.

STRUCTURE OF COURSE #1: ALLY FUNDAMENTALS AT A GLANCE

	Session #1: Getting started on our journey	Session #2: Unconscious Bias	Session #3: Unearned racial advantage	Session #4: Sustaining our journey
Segment #1	Check-In	Check-In	Check-In	Check-In
Segment #1.25 (optional)	Getting Grounded*			
Segment #1.5 (optional)	Community value reflection	Community value reflection	Community value reflection	Community value reflection
Segment #2	Listening Tips	Discussion on Unconscious Bias Creating Our own stories	Discussion on Unearned Racial Advantage Creating Our own stories	Understanding Conservatives and Liberals
Segment #3	Assessing My Ally Types	Role-play with Asks and Connect Stories	Role-play with Asks and Connect Stories	How shame affects ally work
Segment #4	Understanding Ally Types	Role-play with Connect and Expand stories	Role-play with Connect and Expand stories	Choosing skeptics and allies to prioritize for engagement
Segment #4.5 (optional)	Role model	Role model	Role model	Role model
Segment #5	Preview	Preview	Preview	Refining our stories Reenlist Decision

INTRODUCTION

Each of the four sessions has a Check-In Segment where allies can get grounded emotionally and report to each other about opportunities they had to live out their allyship since the group convened last. In this Guide, the Check-In Segment is explained in detail. To save space in this document, the write-ups of Session 2, 3, and 4 will reference the descriptions provided below.

GET CENTERED

This is a chance for each person to acknowledge and/or set aside any significant recent events that might affect their ability to be fully engaged in the meeting.

TRIUMPHS AND TRIALS

Participants are expected to speak briefly about any recent opportunities they had to show up as an ally using the communications strategies in the Workbook.

ELEMENT #1: GET CENTERED

LEARNING OBJECTIVES

Build a sense of common community.

Provide an opportunity for people to raise recent events that might affect their ability to be fully present.

Give a chance for people to ask for and/or receive emotional support from others around important events that are affecting them.

WHAT TO SAY TO INITIATE THE PROCESS

At the start of every meeting, our intention is to have a brief Check-In about our progress toward more effective engagements as allies since we last met.

We have been encouraged to think about two core questions:
- *How many opportunities have you had since we met to use the methods of the project?*

> • *How well did you leverage those opportunities to forward your own practice as an ally?*
>
> *My suspicion is that if we honestly examine the time between the sessions, most of us will find moments that might be called Triumphs and others that we might call Trials.*
>
> *Before we get to our Triumphs and Trials, I want to create a space for folks to convey to the group any larger developments in their lives that might be affecting their ability to use these techniques or even just to be focused this evening.*
>
> *Has anyone here had an event in their lives that is so impactful as to affect you in this moment?*
>
> *Have there been any events in our collective culture that have affected you so much that we should process them briefly before we focus in on the task at hand?*

GROUP PROCESS

Give room for any comments. Make sure that people who need emotional support get it, if only briefly. In a small group, this may be an extended conversation.

ELEMENT #2: TRIUMPHS AND TRIALS ELEMENT

LEARNING OBJECTIVES

Reinforce the sense of community and common purpose.
Provide an accountability check.
Document lessons from trying to use methods in the field.

WHAT TO SAY

> *In addition to getting centered emotionally, we will do the Check-In in a way that will give us a chance to share some lessons each of us may have learned since we last met. I suggest we start this habit immediately.*

INTRODUCTION

My suggestion is that we jot down a quick note that will help us briefly share comments on the following question: 1) Briefly describe a moment that might be called one of Triumph, where you were proud of the way that you responded to a racially problematic statement. 2)Briefly describe a moment that might be called a moment of Trial, where you were not particularly proud of your behavior as an anti-racism ally.

GROUP PROCESS
- After people jot their notes down, have a discussion.
- Consider starting with the failures, then moving to successes.
- To the extent possible, note any alignment or disconnect between the tenants of the project and the participants' experiences.

NOTE TO GROUP LEADERS
If a particularly useful intriguing trial moment comes up, consider probing the group about how an ally who is highly expert with the methods might have handled the situation differently. If you do this, be careful to not let the conversation go so long that it keeps everyone from checking in or blocks something else later in the agenda.

ALLY CONVERSATION TOOLKIT
(ACT) DISCUSSION GROUP
LEADERS GUIDE—COURSE #1

SESSION #1 — BEGINNING OUR COLLECTIVE JOURNEY AS ALLIES

LEARNING OBJECTIVES
- Establish norms for the group.
- Build a sense of community.
- Connect/reconnect people with the core sensibility and approach of the project.
- Begin the practice of reflecting on recent Triumphs and Trials.
- Get participants to identify Listening Tips they will experiment with until Session 2.
- Have participants see themselves in light of the Ally Response Types.
- Clarify the assignments to be done before the next meeting.

INSTRUCTIONS TO GIVE THE GROUP BEFORE THE LESSON
- If participants are not bringing the entire Workbook to the session, they should bring the following p.s:
  - » pp. 9-11
  - » pp. 38-43
  - » pp. 58-79
  - » pp. 87-90
  - » pp. 231-233
- In addition to bringing those p.s to the meeting, they should do the following before the meeting:
  - » Complete the Ally Response Tool on pp. 44-45
  - » Read pp. 9-17 and 58-59
- In addition, pp. 38-43 and 60-79 should be thought of as suggested reading.

SESSION ONE

BEGINNING OUR COLLECTIVE JOURNEY AS ALLIES

PRE-WORK PREPARATION BY THE DISCUSSION GROUP LEADER

- Think about how you would briefly communicate your motivation for being a group leader.
- Choose which Listening Tips have the most appeal to you. (The tips are on pp. 38-43). If you have actually tried them, be prepared to share your experience of the tip.
- Complete the Ally Response Tool (participants will do this during the session) on pp. 44-45.
- Read over all of the long-form descriptions of the Ally Types (pp. 46-54).

The following is a suggestion for an opening process for the course, whether the start of the course is Session 0 or Session 1.

COURSE OPENER: WELCOME, COMMUNITY BUILDING, AND ESTABLISHING NORMS

OBJECTIVES

- To help participants feel connected to each other and to the overall group purpose
- To begin the practice of creating a space of mutual accountability
- To begin a conversation about what the group can expect from each others

WHAT TO SAY

Welcome, thanks for being a part of this discussion group. I am the group leader, but this is OUR group. I am doing it because of my commitment to racial equity.

It is important for us all to take responsibility for creating a good experience for ourselves and others. I have some guidance from ACT that I am happy to share openly if anyone has any concerns. My hope is that we can work out any concerns like good allies collaborating for a greater cause.

Our main tasks today will be:
- *Beginning to get to know each other.*
- *Checking in with our level of progress in using these methods.*
- *Acquainting or reacquainting ourselves with the empathy-based approaches of ACT.*
- *Understanding our Ally Response Type.*
- *Clarifying which Listening Tips we are going to experiment with before out next meeting.*

BASIC INTRODUCTIONS

OBJECTIVES

- To allow people to get a sense of each other.
- To create some moments when people are laughing and/or smiling together.

WHAT TO SAY TO START THE INTRODUCTIONS

Before we go any further, let's do a round of introductions. I suggest that your personal introduction follow this format:
- *Name and occupation*
- *Motivation for being a part of the discussion group*
- *Most fun thing you have done/will do within one month of today (past activities or future plans)*

GROUP PROCESS

Go around the group and let everyone introduce themselves.

NOTE TO GROUP LEADERS

Since two of the three items require a little thought, it may make sense to give people thirty to sixty seconds of silence before the first person shares. This will allow people time to think of an answer in advance and not be searching for it when it is their turn to speak.

If someone's introduction is much longer than others, thank them for their willingness to share, but offer that there is a need to keep the introductions somewhat brief so that the group can progress to other items.

At this point, you should consider handing out a copy of the Discussion Group Norms and Expectations, then briefly review the document with the participants.

DISCUSSION GROUP NORMS AND EXPECTATIONS

- The ACT project does not give an extensive list of instructions for these groups. We are expected to use our common sense and our prior experience of being in groups to help us create good experiences for ourselves.

- This is the Ally Fundamentals Course (also known as Course #1), which comprises four sessions, including this one. The hope is that some or all of us will be so inspired and enthused about our growth as allies that we will want to sign up for more collective learning as part of our ally journey. Course #2—Hot Topics—is five sessions and Course #3—Healing History—is six sessions. At the end of Course #1 we will determine who is interested in continuing this community of learning.

- The expectation is that each participant has purchased the White Ally Toolkit Workbook and will bring the book to the meeting or the relevant p.s that we will be addressing. The project website (www.allyconversationtoolkit.com) will list the p.s from the PDF version that are suitable for each session.

- Our sessions will go more efficiently if everyone has done the short readings and exercises assigned for the upcoming sessions. You should still come to the meetings if you have not done the reading or exercises.

- At every session, we will do a brief Check-In to get centered for our work. We will also talk to each other about the opportunities we may have had to use the methods suggested by this project.

- As a general matter, we will presume that, except perhaps for counteracting the most vile and violent racists, empathy-based approaches are more effective than strategies based on confrontation and verbal combat when encountering racism skeptics.

- The group will be directed to some video content that will be useful (but not absolutely necessary) to watch before each session. We may make watching videos part of our learning during the meetings.

SEGMENT #1: CHECK-IN

LEARNING OBJECTIVES

- Build a sense of common community.
- Provide an opportunity for people to raise recent events that might affect their ability to be fully present.
- Give a chance for people to ask for and/or receive emotional support from others around important events that are affecting them.
- Reinforce sense of community and common purpose.
- Provide accountability check.
- Document lessons from trying to use methods in the field.

NOTE TO GROUP LEADERS

Since this is the first meeting, it is important to establish a tone that sets the precedent for future meetings. Specifically, your goal is to strike a good balance between following an agenda that leads to completion of the learning objectives, and responding to the realities of what is happening in the room with the participants, something that cannot be predicted.

This balance is particularly relevant to the Check-In process, which has two elements and was reviewed previously: 1) Get Centered, which helps participants clear away factors in their awareness that might undermine their participation, and 2) Triumphs and Trials, which is a moment of accountability where participants look directly at how many opportunities they have recently had to use the skills of the Workbook.

One critical task is to let the group give support to any participant who is grappling with something that is consuming their focus, but not to let the giving of that support go on so long that your overall meeting agenda is derailed.

In this first meeting, it may not make sense to do the Check-In Element 1: Get Centered since the group has not met previously. However, it does make sense do the Check-In Element 2: Triumphs and Trials. Follow the sequence that has been outlined above.

SEGMENT #1.25: GETTING GROUNDED (OPTIONAL)

LEARNING OBJECTIVES

- Provide multiple rationales about why empathy-based strategies work better and why white allies should be the people to use them.

- Provide information about the level of group buy-in on empathy-based strategies.

- Increase buy-in to empathy-based strategies, if group buy-in is low.

- Create group bonding around the value of empathy, if group buy-in is high.

- Review the RACE Method, the core approach promoted by this project.

NOTE TO GROUP LEADERS

The White Ally Toolkit Introduction Workshops are intended to provide anti-racism allies with an immersive experience that encourages participants to emphasize empathy-based strategies for engaging racism skeptics, provide information justifying these strategies, and to give a taste of how it feels to practice such strategies. Working through the Getting Grounded segment in and of itself would not be effective as a workshop, but should provide enough grounding so that participants can effectively engage the course.

The Getting Grounded segment lasts forty-five to ninety minutes. In all likelihood, the more familiar that the participants are with empathy-based strategies, the shorter this segment needs to be. One important decision that group leaders need to make is whether it is best for the group to add this session to Session 1 or to make this session into a separate meeting — Session 0—that happens before Session 1. In these cases, you should use a brief course introduction process similar to that outlined above.

SEGMENT STRUCTURE

- Have participants reflect on their buy-in to empathy-based approaches.

- Poll the group on their level of buy-in to empathy-based methods of engagement.

- If the collective buy-in is low, encourage participants to reflect on their experiences of effective and ineffective persuasion.

- If the collective buy-in is high, reinforce existing level of buy-in to empathy-based strategies.

- Explain the RACE Method and the reasons why white allies should use it.

PRELIMINARY WORK BEFORE THE SESSION

Before the session, you should encourage the participants to familiarize themselves with the three sets of ideas, which can be found in the Workbook:

- Arguments why white allies should take on the work of talking to other whites—pp. 13-17.

- What science says about empathy-based methods—pp. 9-12.

- The basic approach of the RACE Method—pp. 58-59.

Note that there are videos on the ACT website that review these ideas.

NOTE TO GROUP LEADERS

A primary task for the Session 0 is to get sufficient buy-in to the approach of using empathetic listening as a primary strategy for engaging racism skeptics. Your goal is to give some room for the expression of doubts and questions about this approach. However, you don't want to get bogged down in debates about empathy-based versus argument-based approaches.

If you have personal experiences relevant to the effectiveness of empathy-based strategies in engaging people who have racially problematic views, it may be helpful to reflect on these experiences before the meeting. The group may be best served if you can relate an anecdote that embodies the power of empathetic listening.

ELEMENT #1: GETTING PARTICIPANTS TO REFLECT ON THEIR LEVEL OF BUY-IN

LEARNING OBJECTIVES

- Reconnect participants to their motivation for learning about empathy-based approaches.

- Surface the fact that they may encounter allies who are likely to question this strategy.

WHAT TO SAY TO INTRODUCE BUY-IN TO EMPATHETIC LISTENING

Being an effective ally can be difficult, and it is important to stay motivated through the challenges of trying to use empathy-based approaches when dealing with racism skeptics. Sometimes doing this will be difficult, and you may even be criticized by anti-racism allies you respect for being "too soft on racists."

Such conversations can be difficult and demotivating, so it is useful for us to connect with our core motivations around this way of being an agent for change. No matter how long you have thought like this, it is important to be clear and to be ready to articulate one or two key reasons you wanted to participate in this process of learning empathy-based responses to racially problematic viewpoints.

GROUP PROCESS

- Give everyone one to two minutes to jot down why they wanted to participate in a group learning process focused on using empathy-based strategies to influence people about racism.

- Before the first person goes, remind people that the plan is to give this process about fifteen minutes, and leave room for some discussion, not just reporting-in. The group will need to share the time.

- If a clock is not visible, tell them you will give them a halftime notification, as well as five- and two-minute warnings.

- Suggest that the group try to speak honestly, listen to each other deeply, and be open to finding both similarities and differences.

WHAT TO SAY TO WRAP UP

I am glad that people shared their struggles and challenges in being allies who are committed to empathy-based strategies. One of the reason I am involved in this is because I think that each of us can grow stronger as part of a learning community.

ELEMENT #2: POLLING ON LEVEL OF BUY-IN TO EMPATHY-BASED APPROACHES

LEARNING OBJECTIVES

- Let everyone see the general level of buy-in to empathy-based approaches in the group.

NOTE TO GROUP LEADERS

This process will help you decide whether your next step is to 1) try to reinforce the wisdom that empathy-based approaches work better or 2) build on the existing buy-in on this issue and help participants see the alignment between their wisdom about these strategies and the approaches of this project.

WHAT TO SAY TO SET UP THE POLLING EXERCISE

Before we go any further, let's take the pulse of the group to see our general level of buy-in to empathy-based approaches.

For the sake of this short process, let's imagine that there are two basic styles of communication around differences in perspective, especially when the topic is an important idea about racism or similarly controversial ideas about how the world works.

The lecture or argument style emphasizes making your points strongly and refuting the most vulnerable points of your conversation partner.

The listening or empathy-based style emphasizes trying to understand where your conversation partner is coming from and trying to build on whatever common ground you might have.

Let's define a scale of our level of confidence versus skepticism about the idea that empathy-based approaches are superior to argument-based approaches. For our scale, suppose that "1" represents a good deal of skepticism about whether such approaches are more effective and that "10" represents strong confidence that empathy-based strategies are more effective.

Think about where your personal level of skepticism/confidence regarding empathy-based strategies lies. We should all be honest and not alter our answers. There is no judgment here.

GROUP PROCESS
- Go around the group and hear everyone's number.

NOTE TO GROUP LEADERS
The results of this quick group pulse-taking should influence what you do next. If the level of group buy-in to empathy-based approaches is relatively low (e.g. a sizable portion of the group has buy-in levels of six or less), you could consider how you will fortify buy-in to empathy-based approaches.

Don't spend a lot of group time on arguments about whether empathy-based approaches are best. If buy-in is low but your intuition is that the group will not subsequently be bogged down with arguments, it may not be necessary to fortify the buy-in on empathic strategies.

If your assessment is that the buy-in to empathic approaches is low enough to merit fortification, you should consider doing segment 2A.
If your assessment is that the buy-in to empathic approaches does not need to be reinforced, you should consider doing segment 2B.

ELEMENT #2A: GETTING PARTICIPANTS TO REFLECT ON THEIR EXPERIENCES OF PERSUASION

LEARNING OBJECTIVE
Help participants examine their actual experience of different persuasion strategies.

NOTE TO GROUP LEADERS

Despite the results of the polling of the group, remember that this discussion group will be highlighting empathy-based approaches. The result will not alter the sequence of activities presented in this guide except for this process described just below.

At some point, you may need to ask skeptical participants to set aside their questions about empathic approaches, and use the entire course as a chance to engage in a personal experiment about whether empathy-based strategy work better.

WHAT TO SAY TO GET PARTICIPANTS TO REFLECT ON PAST EXPERIENCES OF PERSUASION

Many groups like this are based on a shared sense that empathy-based approaches for engaging racism skeptics work better than other communication strategies. Clearly, in our group, we have some variation in our level of buy-in to this idea.

I suggest we unpack our perspectives by writing a few notes about some moments where persuasion was attempted, and we can have a conversation about what our experience tells us about what tends to work and what does not work.

For this exercise, we are going to use ppp. 230 to 232 of the Workbook to make notes on four types of experiences:
- *Times when someone was the target of an argument-style conversation, and their views actually became more hardened*
- *Times when you witnessed someone who was the target of an argument-style conversation, and they changed their views*
- *Times when someone used an empathy-based approach with you, and you made some adjustments in your view*
- *Times when you used an empathy-based approach with someone else, and they made some changes in their view*

We will all take a few notes on some experiences, then talk about them.

GROUP PROCESS

- Have participants turn to pp. 231-233 and jot some notes about their experiences.

- Facilitate a discussion about people's experience of these types of experiences.

- Take verbal note of the number of stories in each category and explore with the group the implications of these proportions.

ELEMENT #2B: REINFORCE THE EXISTING LEVEL OF BUY-IN TO EMPATHY-BASED STRATEGIES

LEARNING OBJECTIVES

- Help participants connect with important insights about strategies that are effective with racism skeptics

NOTE TO GROUP LEADERS

Participants in discussion groups are highly likely to have experiences that illustrate the way that empathy-based strategies tend to be more effective, even if they have not figured out a way to utilize them consistently.

If there are more than six people, it may be useful to divide up the group to ensure that each person has a chance to speak. If you divide into two small groups, subgroups should provide a brief report to the entire group.

While you should not let this exercise overwhelm other processes, bonding over their frustration of ineffective strategies and their appreciation of effective ones can be a powerful way of building a sense of community in the group.

VIDEO SUPPLEMENT

The website for this project (www.allyconversationtoolkit.com) has a number of short videos where allies reflect on strategies they have learned that are helpful and not helpful when trying to reach racism skeptics.

WHAT TO SAY TO CLOSE THE DISCUSSION

This project has found that there is a high degree of alignment between empathy-based approaches and what allies have discovered about what works when talking to racism skeptics.

You are invited to look at the lessons on the project site to see a number of conclusions about what white allies have reported about what works and does not.

NOTE TO GROUP LEADERS

Clarify that the group is going to go forward based on the idea that empathy-based strategies work better. At some point, it might be useful to say something along the lines of:

We are going to thoroughly examine what actually happens when we try methods based on empathy and listening. But we are not going to question the core premise that these methods tend to work better.

If you are unclear and need some more reinforcement, there are some exercises on pp. 230-232 of the Workbook. At the end of the meeting, we can have a conversation about whether there is some way for the project to support your doing this background work to fortify your beliefs. In the meantime, we are not going to take up group time debating this point.

ELEMENT #3: EXPLAIN THE RACE METHOD AND THE REASONS WHY WHITE ALLIES SHOULD USE IT

LEARNING OBJECTIVES

- To review some scientific findings that validate the use of empathy-based approaches.
- To review some arguments about why white allies should bear more of the burden of helping skeptics revisit their views on racism.
- To review the substantive components of the RACE method of managing conversations about race/racism.

KEY TOPICS

Topic 1: Why white allies should take on the work of persuasion of skeptics.

Topic 2: The scientific justification of empathy-based strategies.

Topic 3: The RACE method of engaging skeptics.

Note that for each of these topics, there is a discussion in the Workbook as well as video support materials.

NOTE TO GROUP LEADERS

Ideally, you will have given the participants advance notice to read the sections of the Workbook that will give them background relevant to the key topics. It is a good idea to review the main points, whether they have done the reading or not.

You will need to make a decision about how you bring the attention of the participants to the core ideas before your conversation. Options include:
Watch the relevant videos on the ACT website.
Give people eight to ten minutes to read the relevant pages of the Workbook.
Review the main points at a high level.

Separate the discussion of Topic 3 above (the RACE method) from the discussions of Topics 1 and 2. Make a decision about whether you will have a short discussion after separate presentations of Topic 1 and Topic 2, or whether you want to present both of them together.

WHAT TO SAY TO OPEN THE DISCUSSION

This approach builds upon three ideas (and where you can find information in the Workbook:

- *There are good reasons why white allies should do more of the persuasion work than they are now—pp. 13-17.*
- *There are good scientific reasons for people using empathy-based strategies for persuading people out of their skepticism that racism is real—pp. 9 -12.*
- *The RACE method is well situated to integrate the scientific findings into a strategy that allies can use—pp. 58-59.*

The goal of this next section is to have a brief discussion where we can share how we feel about each of these points.

GROUP PROCESS

Bring the group's attention to Topics 1 and 2, then discuss their perspective on this material. Some discussion questions might include:

- Which of these arguments most resonates with you?

- Are there any arguments you find yourself inclined to disagree with?

- Have you ever discussed these issues with allies before, and if so, what did you get out of these conversations?

After some conversation, bring the group's attention to Topic 3 (the RACE method). Some discussion questions might include:

- What questions do you have about this method or how to use it?

- Do you have any prior experience with using strategies related to these methods? How did that go?

- Which aspects of this method do you feel will be easiest or most difficult to actually do?

- How easy or difficult is it to imagine using this method on non-racial topics? Are there other opportunities to practice before our next conversation about race/racism?

SEGMENT #1.5: VALUES DEEPEN OUR ENGAGEMENT (OPTIONAL)

The inspiring quotations and excerpts highlighting this session's underlying value—Commitment—is provided in the appendices.

SEGMENT #2: LISTENING TIPS

LEARNING OBJECTIVES

- Participants reflect on which Listening Tips they are most drawn to.

- Participants make a commitment to trying at least one Listening Tip before the next meeting.

WHAT TO SAY TO PROMPT THEIR ENGAGEMENT OF THE WORKSHEETS

As you probably remember from the workshop, the methods of this project are grounded in empathetic listening. Thus, it is vital that each of us learn more about the steps we must take to become better listeners.

Even though you might have done this in the workshop, I want to encourage you to take a look again at the Listening Tips on pp. 40-42 of the Workbook. Circle three to four of the tips, including at least one in each of the three categories.

GROUP PROCESS

Give people one to two minutes to circle the tips that they are most drawn to.

WHAT TO SAY TO CATALYZE THE CONVERSATION

If you have thought about which Listening Tips tend to work better for you, briefly say this to the group. Make sure to state not only what tips worked, but also what you were paying attention to that helped you conclude which tip(s) worked best.

After offering your own perspectives, open the conversation with this question: Has anybody ever tried any of these Listening Tips, whether the topic was about race or not? If so, were there any findings that it would be useful to lift up for the group?

NOTE TO GROUP LEADERS

In the discussion, you may want to gently probe participants to say how they noticed that a tip was working or not. Your objective in this exercise is to move participants to the mindset of wanting to try different Listening Tips and then noticing what tends to work on them. A key goal of the conversation is fostering more self-reflection about what works and what does not.

WHAT TO SAY TO CLOSE THE CONVERSATION

Perfecting your listening skills is an ongoing process. It is useful to experiment with other tips. You can try using these listening tips on conversations not related to race.

SEGMENT #3: ALLY RESPONSE TYPES - TAKING THE INSTRUMENT

LEARNING OBJECTIVES

- To acquaint/remind them of their Ally Response Type using the Ally Response Instrument.

- To solicit any feedback about how the tool might be improved.

VIDEO SUPPLEMENT

The ACT website has short videos where facilitators in a workshop give instruction to participants about taking the Ally Response Instrument. Feel free to use a video if you want. However, the task is rather simple to execute from your own instruction.

WHAT TO SAY ABOUT WHY WE ARE REVISITING THE ALLY RESPONSE TYPE

Some of you did the Ally Response Type in the workshop, but some may not have.

In the two years of the ACT project, it has become clear that while every ally is a unique person, there are some patterns of responses in how allies respond to situations when people make remarks that are either racist or that deny racism.

Also, sometimes simply becoming more aware of one's tendencies can change them. So you may be different now that when you took the Instrument before.

Our next exercise is to:
- *Answer two questions in the Assessment Tool.*
- *Use a legend to compute a score.*
- *Read the short and/or long descriptions of the type associated with your score.*

VIDEO CONTENT

On the website, you will find two different videos that you may or may not choose to integrate into your process. One of them explains the tool, its purpose, and the instructions. A second one provides a verbal explanation of the Ally Response Types. It is strongly suggested that you play the explanation of the types, since this explanation allows the participants to see how the types relate to each other.

Whether you use the video content, the most important process is the discussion that the group has. The key questions are:

- To what extent do you find the description of your type accurate?

- Are there any useful lessons or insights from thinking about your type?

- Are there any key insights that you think your type might be able to learn from other types?

Then discuss the group findings.

SEGMENT #4: ALLY RESPONSE TYPE - REFLECTING ON THE ALLY TYPES

GROUP PROCESS

- To help allies understand themselves better, the project has developed an Ally Response Assessment Tool. The abbreviated survey instrument on pp. 44-45 should be taken by participants.

- Look at p. 45 and find your type.

- Read the long form description of your type.

- Jot down a number from one to six about the description with one as very accurate and six as very inaccurate

- Have a discussion: What does the description get right about who you are and the challenges ahead for you? What does it get wrong?

- On the ACT website, there is a Discussion Group Leaders Feedback form that is available to download and fill out. Please use it and send it back filled out (preferably as a Word doc but a handwritten sheet filled out and sent as an image is acceptable) so we can help improve the project.

- Discuss this question: Are there important things that the divergent types can learn from each other?

NOTE TO GROUP LEADERS

Given the ways that the types are different, some learning opportunities become clear immediately. For instance:

- Scouts and Cavalry might be able to teach something to Analysts about tapping into deep motivation.

- Undercover Spies might be able to teach something to Analysts about taking action while staying centered.

- Undercover Spies and Reservists might be able to teach something to Scouts and Cavalry about remaining centered after they hear comments.

- Cavalry and Undercover Spies might be able to teach something to Scouts about how they motivate themselves to take action when they don't really feel like doing so.

WHAT TO SAY TO CLOSE THIS SEGMENT AND TRANSITION

At the end of discussion group, we will take the assessment tool again to see if any of us have changed.

SEGMENT #4.5: POTENTIAL ALLY ROLE MODEL

See the appendix for supplemental material that might be used at this point in the session.

SEGMENT #5: PREVIEW OF SESSION #2 (UNCONSCIOUS BIAS), HOMEWORK ASSIGNMENT, AND CLOSING

LEARNING OBJECTIVES

- To get participants excited about the homework that will make the next session most productive.

WHAT TO SAY TO GET THEM MOTIVATED FOR THE HOMEWORK

The next session will focus on developing and practicing Connect and Expand stories about unconscious bias.

The homework is going to be filling out the forms and developing your stories. You don't need to actually develop the stories, but it would be best if you looked at the prompt questions and jotted some notes down for the ones that were most relevant to your life. If you want to develop your stories before the session, that is also fine.

To get some momentum going, let's spend a few minutes looking over the prompt questions on pp. 91-92 that you might ask a skeptic and that are presented to get you thinking.

GROUP PROCESS

- Have participants read over the prompt questions for the Connect and Expand stories (Workbook pp. 87-90).

- Discussion: Does the way these stories differ make sense to you? Do you have a high-level understanding of the kinds of experiences you will try to tap into as the basis of your story?

WHAT TO SAY AS YOU GIVE THEM THE HOMEWORK ASSIGNMENT

Please bring pp. 87 to 99 to our next meeting.

Our session the next time will be best spent if you have done the following before we meet:
- *Read Module on Unconscious Bias (Workbook, pp. 87–99).*
- *Read primer section on Unconscious Bias (Workbook, pp. 188–193).*
- *Take notes on connect and expand stories on unconscious bias. Also, please bring pp. 87 to 95.*

If you are an overachiever, you can also:
- *Create and perhaps practice a Connect story on unconscious bias.*
- *Create and perhaps practice an Expand story about unconscious bias.*

NOTE TO GROUP LEADERS

- If you have personal anecdotes, share them at some point in the conversation.

- Leave enough time for announcements and any other statements that people want to share.

- Remind the group that it may be useful for them to practice the Listening Tips when in conversations on other topics.

- Confirm the next meeting time and place.

- Adjourn.

ALLY CONVERSATION TOOLKIT
(ACT) DISCUSSION GROUP
LEADERS GUIDE—COURSE #1

SESSION #2 — UNCONSCIOUS BIAS

LEARNING OBJECTIVES

- Reinforce norms for the group, such as Check-In and Triumphs and Trials.

- Build on the sense of community.

- Experience a brief conversation about unconscious bias.

- Help the group understand the way using the RACE method creates a different interaction compared to the ones that allies and skeptics typically have about unconscious bias.

- Develop and practice Connect and Expand stories about unconscious bias.

- Clarify the assignments to be done before the next meeting.

Ideally, the preparation by the leader for the session should include:

- Read the Module on Unconscious Bias (Workbook, pp. 87–99), including jotting notes about personal anecdotes.

- Read primer section on Othering (Workbook pp. 182-187).

- Read the Primer section on Unconscious Bias (Workbook, pp. 188-193), and be prepared to provide a high-level verbal summary of the key ideas.

- Create and practice a Connect story about unconscious bias.

- Create and practice an Expand story about unconscious bias.

- Be prepared to briefly explain your key decisions constructing your anecdote.

- Bring copies of the role-play instructions for the Connect and Expand stories. Bring enough copies for every participant and yourself. These instructions are at the end of this Session description.

Ideally, participants should have been assigned the following homework:

- Read Module on Unconscious Bias (Workbook, pp. 87–99).
- Read primer section on Unconscious Bias (Workbook, pp. 188–193).
- Take notes on Connect and Expand stories.
- Optional – create and practice Connect story.
- Optional – create and practice Expand story.

SEGMENT #1: CHECK-IN

Follow the sequence of the Check-In, including both the Getting Centered and the Triumphs and Trials, that was outlined earlier in this document.

SEGMENT #1.5: QUOTATIONS AND EXCERPTS THAT VALIDATE AND INSPIRE (OPTIONAL)

See appendices for content for specific populations.

SEGMENT #2: EXPLORING PERSPECTIVES ON UNCONSCIOUS BIAS

LEARNING OBJECTIVE

- Get participants to tune into their thoughts about unconscious bias.
- Clarify the way that creating and deploying a Connect story will diffuse conflicts that skeptics may expect.
- Have participants practice asking an experience question related to a skeptic's disbelief that unconscious bias matters.
- Have people create and practice a Connect story about unconscious bias.

WHAT TO SAY

In a few minutes, we are going to turn to creating personal anecdotes about unconscious bias. Before we turn to this task, let's have a brief conversation about this concept.

Is there anyone who feels comfortable summarizing some key takeaways about unconscious bias that we should all keep in mind as we do our work today?

(If no one wants to do it, focus group attention on pp. 188-190. Verbally review the key points on these pages.)

(After the summary, engage the group in the following way:)

Let's just start with two questions:
- *Did anything strike you from the reading that either challenged your thinking about unconscious bias or that reinforced it?*
- *What is your experience of unconscious bias, either directed at you or existing within you in a way that it might have affected your thoughts or behavior?*

GROUP PROCESS
Hear brief comments from the participants.

NOTE TO GROUP LEADER
If this conversation runs out of steam or needs boosting, consider using these additional questions:
- To what extent has your thinking about unconscious bias changed over time?
- How do you think your perspective about unconscious bias compares to most skeptics you know? How does it compare to most allies you know?
- Is there anything difficult to talk about regarding unconscious bias that is useful to acknowledge?

SEGMENT #3: CREATING OUR OWN STORIES RELATED TO UNCONSCIOUS BIAS

LEARNING OBJECTIVES
- Give the group a chance to hear and give feedback on your own Connect and Expand stories.

- Encourage participants to develop their Connect stories.
- Get participants to think about making asks about unconscious bias.
- Have participants practice their asks and Connect stories in a role-play.

NOTE TO GROUP LEADER

It will likely be helpful to crystallize ways that the RACE method varies from a pattern of talking about race/racism that is common between allies and skeptics. If you think that there is a widely shared understanding of and appreciation for the RACE method, you may not need to do any additional clarification. However, some groups have found that a short presentation of how Connect stories shift interactions can help energize the activity of creating them.

WHAT TO SAY TO EXPLAIN HOW CONNECT STORIES ON UNCONSCIOUS BIAS CAN SHIFT INTERACTIONS

Our intention is to have everyone leave our meeting tonight with two stories about unconscious bias—one that is likely to feel validating to a racism skeptic, and one that is likely to challenge the skeptic to expand their thinking.

The following talking points may be helpful to review:

The skeptic's belief that they are colorblind and don't need to spend any time or effort thinking about race is often related to another belief. Namely, that they should be given credit for not absorbing more bigoted messages that commonly circulate among the white population.

Often, this desire to be acknowledged for not being more racist is met by anti-racism allies with a message that feels to them like "Don't congratulate yourself. In fact, you are complacent and are not doing enough."

The goal of the RACE method is to create a different way of responding to their claim of colorblindness and the underlying desire to be acknowledged for not being consciously bigoted. Instead of conveying, "You don't deserve credit, and you are not doing enough" your goal is to convey, "That's great, I have done something similar, and there is also more work that we all should do." Your Connect story conveys that you give them credit for doing some important work on race, while your subsequent Expand story conveys that there is more to be done.

The first thing we are going to do is to create our Connect story. Then we will review possibilities for asking follow-up questions when somebody says that the only racism that matters is conscious bigotry. Then we will practice the question and the story during a role-play.

WHAT TO SAY AS YOU MODEL YOUR CONNECT AND EXPAND STORIES AS MODELS FOR THE GROUP

I have done some preliminary work on my Connect and Expand stories for unconscious bias. Imagine that I am in a conversation with someone who says they are colorblind or that unconscious bias is just an idea floated to make some people feel bad. After asking them a question to get them to say more about their experiences related to this belief, I might tell them these two stories in order to try to first agree with them, then to try to invite them to new thinking.

(Tell your Connect story)

After a brief pause to recognize the agreement between myself and the skeptic, I might proceed to my Expand story, which goes like this:

(Tell your Expand story)

GROUP PROCESS
Solicit feedback about the stories. If anyone criticizes the stories, do not get defensive, but you may want to explain why you made the choices you did.

After fielding answers, discuss some key decisions that you made as your created your anecdote. Some issues might include:

- Did each of the stories make sense to you as Connect and Expand stories?

- Given your objectives in the storytelling, were there aspects of the experience that you might otherwise tell that you left out to streamline it?

- Given your objectives, were there details of the story that you emphasized to help make your point?

WHAT TO SAY TO INTRODUCE THE PROCESS OF CREATING A CONNECT STORY

Next, we will spend a few minutes thinking about our recollections so we can choose a situation that seems most suitable for a Connect anecdote. Turn to pp. 88-91 for the prompts to help you create your stories.

NOTE TO GROUP LEADER

After about four minutes, it may be helpful to remind the group that it would be counterproductive to spend so much time trying to find the perfect story that we don't have time to practice telling it.

WHAT TO SAY TO PREPARE THE GROUP FOR THE ROLE-PLAY

We are about to do a role-play so that each of us can practice our storytelling to a skeptic. You can use the time when you are in the role of a skeptic to practice your story telling. Feel free to make up a story from a skeptic, or to repeat one that you have heard. But you can also use your time as a skeptic to get one more opportunity to practice your Connect story.

The difference between telling your story as an ally and as yourself is simple. Just change the takeaway. When you play the role of a skeptic, you can "supercharge" the takeaway so much that it becomes spurious, and perhaps even laughable.

For instance: Suppose your story is about how your mother used to teach you to fear black people and you resisted that message and don't teach your children that. In the role of a skeptic, tell the same story but add a supercharged conclusion. You might have the same set-up and key moment but add the following takeaway: Everyone you know who had a racist mom does not now teach racism to their children. This (you might say as a skeptic) proves that our culture has become colorblind.

Before we break into pairs for the role-play, let's briefly review some suggestions about making asks.

NOTE TO GROUP LEADERS

Before the role-play, the next step is to have the group briefly familiarize themselves with some different possibilities for questions that might be appropriate for further discussion.

WHAT TO SAY TO INTRODUCE OPTIONS FOR THE ASK

We are almost ready to do the role-play that goes through the Connect story. Before we do, let's take a quick look at the questions on p. 90 to 91 of the Workbook. What you see there are some specific ways that you might follow up with an experience-based question after a person makes it apparent that they are unfamiliar with the idea of unconscious bias or are skeptical about it. Take a quick look and note if any questions strike you as particularly usable or not.

GROUP PROCESS

- Group silently reads the five questions starting at the bottom of p. 90.
- Group discusses their perspective on the usability of the questions.

WHAT TO SAY TO TRANSITION TO ROLE-PLAY

(Hand out the instructions for the role-play through the Connect step)

We will now turn to our role-play. You can see the instructions for the process on the handout. Let's quickly review the key steps of the role-play instruction sheet.

The next task is to form into pairs. If possible, form a pair with someone you do not know and have not worked with much at previous meetings.

NOTE TO GROUP LEADERS

If you have an odd number of group participants including yourself, consider the best way for you to balance your need to practice your stories and the need for others in the group to practice theirs. If you really need to practice, you might decide to join a pair group and do your storytelling quickly, so the other members of the trio get most of the time for their practice. You also might decide to not use this time to practice and spend the time monitoring other people in the group.

Tell the group that this Connect story role-play exercise should take no more than about four minutes for each person.

When the pairs have completed both rounds of the role-play and debrief, have a brief discussion (five to ten minutes) about the participants' reflections about how the process felt. Possible questions include:

- What were the lessons or surprises you learned from the experience, either playing yourself or the skeptic?
- Did anything happen in the process that you think others will benefit from hearing about?
- What are the key lessons about managing the conversation to this point?
    » If possible, take notes on key lessons so that you can turn them into ACT.

SEGMENT #4: PREPARE AN EXPAND STORY, DO A FULL ROLE-PLAY OF THE RACE METHOD ABOUT UNCONSCIOUS BIAS

LEARNING OBJECTIVES

- Each participant prepares an Expand story.

- Participants practice Ask, Connect, and Expand steps through a role-play.

WHAT TO SAY TO TRANSITION TO EXPAND STORIES

Practicing the RACE method only through the Connect step can feel weird because you don't get the chance to make the important effort to expand the skeptic's thinking. While this might be frustrating, sometimes this happens. There are times when a situation shifts, and the conversation stops after the Connect story. It is important that you stay committed to finishing the RACE method. But this may not happen in the same conversation.

We will turn next to creating Expand stories. This may feel easier than creating a Connect story, since you may have some "go to" stories that you think are compelling on this topic. The opportunity here is to reexamine their effectiveness. Remember, you are going to be talking to someone who tends to believe that the most important thing is being "colorblind" and who does not understand or perhaps doubts the idea of unconscious bias.

GROUP PROCESS

- Each member of the group fills out the worksheet on pp. 93-94 that focuses on creating an Expand story about unconscious bias.

- Leader reviews the role-play instruction sheet that goes through the Expand story.

- After you assess that most participants are ready for the role-play, inform the group that they will work with a different partner.

- As before, monitor the progress of the pairs. If you have to be in a pair because of numbers, make sure a different person is your partner as you play the role of the skeptic for them.

- Conduct the role-play, giving each person about eight minutes before switching roles.

WHAT TO SAY TO HELP THE GROUP DEBRIEF THE ROLE-PLAY

- *What were the lessons or surprises you learned from the experience, either playing yourself or the skeptic?*
- *How would you assess the smoothness/awkwardness of transitioning from the Connect to Expand stories?*
- *Did anything happen in the process that you think others will benefit from hearing about?*
- *Now that you have practiced both, how would you contrast your intended takeaways from each type of story?*
- *Was there any difference in how you did the exercise because you knew you could get to your expand story?*

NOTE TO GROUP LEADERS

If you have time, you can close this process by having a brief encounter about their readiness to deploy these stories in the wild. The following is a process for doing that, which is different than simply asking, "Who thinks they are ready to use their stories?"

Option 1: Open Discussion—Ask the group, "Who thinks they are ready to use their stories?" and "What feelings do you have thinking about doing so?"

Option 2: Private Self-Assessment, Reveal, Discussion—This takes a little longer, but is a potentially richer interaction.

- Have them mentally assess their readiness to use the RACE method with a skeptic the next time they hear a comment reasonably related to unconscious bias.

  - » 1 stands for mostly not ready
  - » 2 stands for almost ready
  - » 3 stands for ready and excited

- Have the group reveal their readiness number all at the same time. Everyone look around at everyone's readiness level.

- If there is time, have a discussion about the readiness they feel and what support they might need to be more ready.

WHAT TO SAY

No matter how ready you feel about talking to a skeptic, it is a good idea to find an ally to have this conversation with so you can practice managing the conversation and telling your stories.

The only way to get better at this is to practice. You will be better the fifth time than the first time, and better the twentieth time than the fifth time. The key is getting started.

SEGMENT #4.5: A POTENTIAL ALLY ROLE MODEL (OPTIONAL)

See appendices for content for specific communities.

SEGMENT #5: PREVIEW OF COMING ATTRACTIONS

LEARNING OBJECTIVES

- Participants assess and reveal their readiness to use the processes in the real world.
- Briefly review the goals of next session.
- Clarify the homework that the participants should do.
- Specify what p.s of the workbook they should bring to Session 3.

WHAT TO SAY

In the next meeting we are going to focus on unearned racial advantage, which is the term that ACT uses to describe what is normally referred to as white privilege. One way to think about unearned advantage is that it captures some of the positive benefits of NOT being in a group that experiences unconscious racial bias on a regular basis.

If anyone has any descriptions of white privilege that they have found compelling—especially if they seem aligned with the perspective taken within this project—feel free to give them to me and I will send them to ACT for possible inclusion as resources for the entire project.

As always, pay attention to whether there are moments when you have a chance to use the skills that we are learning here. Do the best you can to show up well, but if a moment of potential Triumph actually becomes a moment of Trial, don't be too hard on yourself. Take note of what was going on with you; the next meeting will be a time to talk about what happened. All of these moments are learning experiences.

Please bring the pp. 100-111 to the next meeting.

Before the next meeting, please do the following:
- *Read the module text (pp. 100-103), and at least take notes about the questions that seem most relevant.*
- *Read the part of the Workbook that focuses on this topic (pp. 202-207), since it may enhance your thinking.*
- *Make some mental notes or some initial written notes about experiences that might be the basis of Connect and Expand stories about unearned racial advantage.*

If you want to be an overachieving ally, you can also:
- *Create and perhaps practice a Connect story about unearned racial advantage.*
- *Create and perhaps practice an Expand story about unearned racial advantage*

Thanks for your continued allyship and I look forward to our next meeting.

PRACTICING THE RACE METHOD THROUGH CONNECT: UNCONSCIOUS BIAS

Choose which person is going play the role of the skeptic first.

PREPARE FOR ROLE-PLAY (TWO MIN):

ALLY PREPARATION TASKS	SKEPTIC PREPARATION TASKS
Review worksheet, mentally rehearse your Connect story	Think about what you might say to further amplify your belief with some additional belief statements.
Consider trying a different Listening Tip than you have used before (pp. 40-42 of the Workbook) Notice how doing the tip affects you.	Mentally rehearse a story that a skeptic might tell to justify their view. (Consider modifying your own Connect story as a possibility.)
Remember, this is just practice. Use this as a learning experience.	Remember that you are not going for the Oscar.

EXECUTE ROLE-PLAY (FOUR MIN):

	ALLY ROLE-PLAY ACTIONS	SKEPTIC ROLE-PLAY ACTIONS
1		The skeptic reads a version of the statement. "I don't have to worry about being racist because I am colorblind."
2	Get the skeptic to say a bit more about their beliefs. Try something like: "That is an interesting point of view. Could you say more about what you think about that?"	
3		Skeptic expands by giving more belief statements.
4	Make an Ask: "Tell me some experience of yours that further confirms your view."	
5		Skeptic tells a story/anecdote.
6	Ally listens empathetically to make the Skeptic feel truly heard.	Skeptic tunes in to how much they feel truly heard by the ally.
7	Ally creates a transition and brings up their own Connect story that relates to some piece of the embedded beliefs of the skeptic.	

DEBRIEFING THE ROLE-PLAY (FOUR MINUTES):

ALLY DISCUSSION QUESTIONS	SKEPTIC DISCUSSION QUESTIONS
How did your Listening Tip work? How did hearing the skeptic's story feel?	How much did your partner make you feel heard during when you told your story?
How did it feel to tell your Connect story?	How did it feel to play the role of the skeptic? What was difficult or easy about it?
What improvements would you like to make on your performance?	Any tips to help the ally sharpen their performance?

SWITCH ROLES AND REPEAT!

PRACTICING THE RACE METHOD, THROUGH EXPAND: UNCONSCIOUS BIAS

Choose which person is going play the role of the skeptic first. You will repeat the preparation steps from a few minutes ago.

EXECUTE ROLE-PLAY (SIX MIN):

	ALLY ROLE-PLAY ACTIONS	SKEPTIC ROLE-PLAY ACTIONS
1		The skeptic reads a version of the statement. "I don't have to worry about being racist because I am colorblind."
2	Ally brings up statement, asks follow-up question to get skeptic to say more about their beliefs.	
3		Skeptic expands on beliefs.
4	Make an Ask to learn about an experience related to the skeptic's beliefs.	
5		Skeptic tells an experience related to the belief.
6	Ally listens empathetically enough to make the skeptic feel truly heard.	Skeptic tunes in to how much they feel truly heard by the ally.
7	Ally creates a transition and brings up their own Connect story that relates to some piece of the embedded beliefs of the skeptic.	
8	After letting the connection exist for a moment, ally creates a transition to signal they are going to tell a second story.	
9	Ally tells Expand story.	Skeptic listens empathetically.
10	Optional: Ally asks whether it is possible for two things that seem the opposite to both be true.	

DEBRIEFING THE ROLE-PLAY (FIVE MIN):

Ally discussion questions	Skeptic discussion questions
What did you do to get in/stay in a listening mode? What lessons, if any, did you learn? How well did it work? How did hearing the skeptic's story feel?	How much did your partner make you feel heard while sharing your experiences?
How did it feel to tell stories? How did your experience of telling the different stories compare?	How did it feel to play the role of the skeptic? What was difficult or easy about it?
What improvements would you like to make on your performance?	Any tips to help the ally sharpen their performance?

SWITCH ROLES AND REPEAT!

ALLY CONVERSATION TOOLKIT
(ACT) DISCUSSION GROUP
LEADERS GUIDE—COURSE #1
SESSION #3 — UNEARNED RACIAL ADVANTAGE (WHITE PRIVILEGE)

LEARNING OBJECTIVES

- Reinforce norms for the group, such as Check-In and Triumphs and Trials.

- Build on the sense of community.

- Help the group understand the way using the RACE method productively creates unexpected interactions between allies and skeptics regarding unearned racial advantage.

- Experience a brief conversation about unearned racial advantage.

- Develop and practice Connect and Expand stories about unearned racial advantage.

- Clarify the assignments to be done before the next meeting.

PREPARATION BY THE LEADER FOR THE SESSION

- Read the Module on Unearned Racial Advantage, including jotting notes about your own personal anecdote, pp. 100-111.

- Read the Primer section on Unearned Racial Advantage, pp. 202-207.

- Create and practice a Connect Story on unearned racial advantage.

- Create and practice an Expand story on unearned racial advantage.

- Be prepared to briefly explain the key decisions you made while constructing your anecdote.

- Bring enough copies of the role-play instructions for the Connect and Expand stories for every participant and yourself.

IDEAL HOMEWORK THAT THE PARTICIPANTS HAVE BEEN ASSIGNED

- Read Module on Unearned Racial Advantage, pp. 100-111.

- Read primer section on Unearned Racial Advantage, pp. 202-207.
- Take notes on connect and expand stories.
- Optional – create and practice Connect story.
- Optional – create and practice Expand story.

SEGMENT #1: CHECK-IN

Follow the sequence of the Check-In, including both the Getting Centered and the Triumphs and Trials, (outlined earlier in this document).

SEGMENT #1.5: QUOTATIONS AND EXCERPTS THAT VALIDATE AND INSPIRE (OPTIONAL)

See appendices for content for specific populations.

SEGMENT #2: EXPLORING OUR PERSPECTIVES ON UNEARNED RACIAL ADVANTAGE (ALSO KNOWN AS WHITE PRIVILEGE)

LEARNING OBJECTIVES
- Review ACT's perspective on unearned racial advantage.
- Discuss the participant's experience and perspective on this topic.
- Clarify the way that creating and deploying a Connect story will diffuse conflicts the skeptic may expect.

WHAT TO SAY TO INTRODUCE THE TOPIC

In a few minutes, we are going to do some written reflective work to develop our Connect and Expand stories on unearned racial advantage. But let's first have a conversation about this topic to stimulate our thinking.

First, I will say a bit about why this conversation is important.

The reason that it is important to create these stories is because of the affect they have on getting people to think about racism. For many racism skeptics, denying they or other white people they care about have some racial advantages goes hand-in-hand with denying that racism exists at all.

By getting a skeptic to acknowledge that there are advantages to being white, you are moving the person one step closer to getting them to see that the continued existence of racism is a reality that runs counter to their own values—especially of fairness.

Here are some additional points about this issue that ACT wanted us to review and briefly consider.

- *There are many advantages of being white in modern America.*
- *These advantages stay largely hidden from the awareness of many white people.*
- *In addition, many people don't like to admit to themselves there are advantages when this is pointed out, somewhat because their lives do not seem easy or "privileged."*
- *Because it appears that both the terms "white" and "privilege" seem to generate resistance, the project tends to use the term "unearned racial advantage." Be mindful, however, that the most important factor in communication is not the precise term, but your success in helping people admit that there are advantages to being white. Don't get hung up on words.*
- *Many people have found that discussing their own journey about realizing that being white has advantages can be an important tool in their persuasion toolkit.*

GROUP PROCESS

- Manage a short conversation about the following three questions:
- Do you have any reactions to my comments about white privilege that might be useful to talk about?
- When you try to convey experiences of yours that embody unearned racial advantage, what comes to your mind?
- Was there a time when you did not agree with the idea of white privilege? How did you come around?

NOTE TO GROUP LEADER

If the conversation runs out of steam, consider these additional questions:

- How hard is it to talk about this? If it is difficult, why?
- Do you have any doubts about the concept that impede you engaging on this? What are they?
- When you read about white privilege, what are the aspects of it that are most striking to you?

SEGMENT #3: CREATING OUR OWN STORIES RELATED TO UNEARNED RACIAL ADVANTAGE AND MAKING ASKS ABOUT IT

LEARNING OBJECTIVES

- Participants explore some key dynamics between allies and skeptics about unearned racial advantage.
- Participants hear your Connect and Expand stories, and observe you absorbing feedback.
- Briefly visit alternative ways of making asks about unearned racial advantage.
- Encourage participants to develop their Connect and Expand stories.
- Have participants practice their stories in a role-play.

WHAT TO SAY TO REVIEW HOW THE RACE METHOD CHANGES INTERACTIONS WITH SKEPTICS

As we know, our intention tonight is to develop two stories about unearned racial advantage—one that is likely to feel validating to a racism skeptic, and one that is likely to challenge the skeptic to expand their thinking.

Let me share a few brief points from the perspective of the ACT project about why and how the RACE method works on discussions of unearned racial advantage. We can make our own assessment of how true or false these ideas sound.

One core reason skeptics resist the idea of white privilege is that they interpret the term to mean that "it is special privileges and not merit that are responsible for the success of themselves and others they care about." When discussing racism with allies, skeptics are typically told this inclination to claim their accomplishments as merited wrong, inadequate, or otherwise flawed.

In a typical argument between a skeptic and an anti-racism ally about privilege, the skeptic's claims that they worked hard for their success or that they faced disadvantages are met with mostly with rejection. What skeptics hear allies tell them—and sometimes what the allies actually say—is that the skeptic is simply wrong (or perhaps even racist) for how they see things.

The strategy of the ACT project is to try to connect with the skeptic before trying to expand their thinking. The connection might be around the idea that life is no cakewalk for many white people; it might be around the related idea that some white people have many advantages over others; it might be the idea that some whites have faced notable disadvantages. None of these or other similar ideas actually obliterate the idea that being white is easier overall than being a person of color.

The goal is to use a personal anecdote that conveys to the skeptic not that they are wrong, but rather that their truth has some validity and also that there is more there more to the story. Your message is that the skeptic understands that an important truth is conveyed by your Connect story, and your message that there is more to the story is conveyed by your Expand story.

Does anyone have any comments or questions about these ideas? Is there anything we need to briefly talk about before we move forward?

(After a brief discussion—remember too that you have many things to cover before the session ends—proceed to the next step.)

In preparing for tonight, I have worked on my own Connect and Expand stories. I will tell them to you now.

Imagine that I am talking to someone who tells me that they don't believe that white privilege is a thing. Also imagine that I have gotten them to tell me an experience story about why they believe this. After that, I might tell them this story:
• *(Leader tells their Connect story)*

Then, after a moment of bonding around our agreement, I might transition to this story.
• *(Leader tells their Expand story)*

GROUP PROCESS
- Leader encourages a short discussion of some suggestions that might make your story even more effective. Possible questions:
- Did each of the stories make sense to you as Connect and Expand stories?
- Do you have any feedback, positive or constructive, about how I might enhance the effectiveness of these stories?
- If I wanted to change the duration of the story, what points might I add or take away?

NOTE TO GROUP LEADER
When discussing the stories, try at some point to convey some options for how you might adapt each story to make it longer or shorter depending on the duration that seems most suitable. If you actually used this story, also convey your perspective on the impact of the story within the setting(s) used.
If anyone criticizes the stories, do not get defensive, but consider that it might be useful to have a short conversation about the advantages and disadvantages of the choices you made.

Without letting the conversation about your stories go on for too long, shift the group's focus to their task of creating a Connect story about unearned racial advantage.

SESSION THREE

GROUP PROCESS

Have each person do the written work on their Connect story. The worksheets for the unearned racial advantage connect story are located on pp. 104-105 of the Workbook.

WHAT TO SAY TO INSTRUCT THE GROUP TO COLLECT THEIR MEMORIES AND THOUGHTS

Next, we will spend a few minutes by thinking about our recollections about a situation when we experienced unearned racial privilege and then going through what we remember and choosing a situation that seems most suitable for a Connect anecdote. Turn to pp. 104-105 for the prompts to help you create your stories.

(At about four minutes, it may be helpful to remind the group that it would be counter-productive to spend so much time trying to find the perfect story that we don't have time to practice telling it.)

NOTE TO GROUP LEADER

The flow of actions follows closely what happened in Session 2. If most of the participants were able to switch between the roles well, it may not be necessary to summarize the text below. If this switching roles proves difficult, however, it may be useful to remind them that their Connect story can be useful when they play the role of the skeptic. If necessary, convey that this process of telling and retelling is something that they can use to refine the story so that it has maximum impact.

WHAT TO SAY TO PREPARE THE GROUP FOR THE ROLE-PLAY

We are about to do a role-play so that each of us can practice our storytelling to someone playing the role of a skeptic. Just like in our last session, you can use the time when you are in the role of a skeptic to practice your story telling. Feel free to make up a story from a skeptic, or to repeat one that you have heard. But you can also use your time as a skeptic to get one more opportunity to practice your Connect story.

As we said in our previous meeting, the difference between telling your story as an ally and as yourself might be very simple. Often, you can just change the takeaway. When you play the role of a skeptic, you can supercharge the takeaway so much that it becomes spurious, and perhaps even laughable.

For instance: Suppose your story is about how you were economically disadvantaged growing up. You can tell the story of your disadvantage, and about how white people in your neighborhood had disadvantages too. Some folks rose above these challenges, and others did not. As an ally, you might deploy this story and conclude with the takeaway that you know that life can be hard for white people. When playing the role of a skeptic, you might tell the same story with the takeaway that that the story is proof that there is no such thing as white privilege.

Just like last time, let us turn to the process of making asks about people's experiences when they make statements about white privilege.

NOTE TO GROUP LEADER

Before you move the group to the role-play, have them spend a few moments looking at possible questions that they could use to follow up on a statement by a skeptic that they don't believe in white privilege.

WHAT TO SAY TO INTRODUCE OPTIONS FOR THE ASK

We are almost ready to do a role-play that goes through the Connect story. Before we do, let's take a quick look at the questions on p. 103 of the Workbook. What you see there are some specific ways that you might follow up with an experience-based question after a person makes it apparent that they are unfamiliar with the idea of unconscious bias or are skeptical about it. Take a quick look and note if any questions strike you as particularly usable or not.

SESSION THREE
UNEARNED RACIAL ADVANTAGE

GROUP PROCESS

- Group silently reads the five questions starting at the bottom of p. 103.

- Group discusses their perspective on the usability of the questions and other ones that might be useful.

WHAT TO SAY TO TRANSITION TO ROLE-PLAY

(Hand out the instructions for the role-play on unearned racial advantage through the Connect step.)

We will now turn next to our role-play. You can see the instructions for the process on the handout. Quickly review the key steps of the role-play instruction sheet. The next task is to divide into pairs. If possible, form a pair with someone you do not know and have not worked with much at previous meetings.

NOTE TO GROUP LEADERS

As with the last session, make a decision about your participation based on your own level of need for more practice, the number of people present, and the needs of the group.

- Tell the group that this connect story role-play exercise should not take more than about four minutes for each person.

- When the pairs have completed both rounds of the role-play and debrief, have a brief discussion (five-ten minutes) about the participants' reflections about how the process felt. Possible questions include:

  » What were the lessons or surprises you learned from the experience, either playing yourself or the skeptic?

  » Did anything happen in the process that you think others will benefit from hearing about?

  » What are the key lessons about managing the conversation to this point?

If possible, take notes on key lessons so that you can turn them into ACT.

SEGMENT #4: CREATE EXPAND STORIES; PRACTICE THE ENTIRE RACE METHOD ON THE TOPIC OF UNEARNED ADVANTAGE

LEARNING OBJECTIVES

- Create and practice an Expand story about unearned racial advantage.

- Practice all phases of the RACE method.

- Assess and increase participant readiness to use these methods in the wild.

WHAT TO SAY TO TRANSITION TO EXPAND STORIES

We will turn next to creating Expand stories. This may feel easier than creating a Connect story, since you may have some "go to" stories that you have already used in conversations about white privilege. If that is the case, the opportunity here is to re-examine how effective these methods would be when talking to someone who does not already believe that unearned racial advantage exists or is significant.

GROUP PROCESS

- Each member of the group fills out the worksheet on pp. 104-108 that focuses on creating an Expand story about unearned racial advantage.

- Leader reviews the role-play instruction sheet that goes through the Expand story.

- As before, monitor the progress of the pairs. If you have to be in a pair because of numbers, make sure a different person is your partner as you play the role of the skeptic for them. As before, you and your partner can spend the rest of the time monitoring the room.

- Conduct the role-play, giving each person eight minutes before switching roles.

WHAT TO SAY TO INTRODUCE THE GROUP PROCESS

(Discuss any lessons from the experience.)

- *What were the lessons or surprises you learned from the experience, either playing yourself or the skeptic?*

- *Did anything happen in the process that you think others will benefit from hearing about?*

Now that you have practiced both, how would you contrast your intended takeaways from each type of story?

DEBRIEF QUESTIONS

- Was there any difference in how you did the exercise because you knew that you could get to your Expand story?

- Was your experience of playing the role of a skeptic any different?

- How would you assess the smoothness/awkwardness of transitioning from the Connect to Expand stories?

NOTE TO GROUP LEADERS

If you have time, you can close this process by having a brief encounter about their readiness to deploy these stories in the wild. The following is a process for doing that, which is different than simply asking, "Who thinks they are ready to use their stories?"

GROUP PROCESS

- Have them mentally assess their readiness to use the RACE method with a skeptic the next time they hear a comment reasonably related to unearned racial advantage/white privilege

  » 1 stands for mostly not ready

  » 2 stands for almost ready

  » 3 stands for ready and excited

- Have the group reveal their readiness number all at the same time. Everyone look around at everyone's readiness level.

- If there is time, have a discussion about the readiness they feel and what support they might need to be more ready.

WHAT TO SAY TO CLOSE THE EXERCISE

No matter how ready you feel about talking to a skeptic, it is a good idea to find an ally to have this conversation with and practice managing the conversation and telling their stories.

The only way to get better at this is to practice. As we said before, you will be better the fifth time than the first time, and better the twentieth time than the fifth time. The key is getting started.

SEGMENT #4.5: A POTENTIAL ALLY ROLE MODEL (OPTIONAL)

See appendices for content targeted to specific populations.

SEGMENT #5: PREVIEW OF COMING ATTRACTIONS

LEARNING OBJECTIVES
- Review the key elements to the final session of this Mini-Course.
- Remind them that we will be discussing the Reenlist decision.
- Clarify the homework and the p.s of the Workbook they should bring next time.

WHAT TO SAY TO REVIEW THE KEY CONTENT IN SESSION #4

The following are the main tasks of Session #4:
- *Examine our experience of and perspective about conservatives.*
- *Think about and discuss skeptics whom it might make sense to focus on at this point in our development.*
- *Have at least a short discussion about the role of shame and how it might affect our interactions with other white people.*
- *See who wants to keep meeting together to further out ally practice.*

At the end of the next session, we will take the pulse of the group to see how many of us want to keep meeting. The next session will be the end of the Fundamentals Mini-Course, but you know that we have done less than half of the book. There are other

Mini-Courses that we could do. Think about whether you want to keep working with some folks in this group.

Make sure that you bring pp. 234-249 with you to our next meeting.

Here is the homework for next time
- *Read commentary about conservatives and liberals—pp. 247-249, pp. 254-257.*
- *Review reading and reflection questions on shame—pp. 236-238*
- *Review reading and reflection questions on choosing skeptics—pp. 239-242.*

WHAT TO SAY TO CLOSE THE SESSION

Before the next meeting, we hope that you practice the skills that we have been developing here. If racism skeptical statements do not come up naturally, you might consider initiating a conversation with a skeptic that is in your orbit. It could be someone in your circle of influence, an acquaintance, or a stranger. You will get more out of this course if you come back each time with an experience or two to reflect on.

PRACTICING THE RACE METHOD THROUGH THE CONNECT STEP
Choose which person is going play the role of the skeptic first.

PREPARE FOR ROLE-PLAY (TWO MIN):

ALLY PREPARATION TASKS	SKEPTIC PREPARATION TASKS
Review worksheet, mentally rehearse your Connect story.	Think about what you might say to further amplify your belief with some additional belief statements.
Consider trying a different Listening Tip than you have used before (pp. 40-42 of the Workbook) Notice how doing the tip affects you.	Mentally rehearse a story that a skeptic might tell to justify their view. (Consider modifying your own Connect story as a possibility.)
Remember, this is just practice. Use this as a learning experience.	Remember that you are not going for the Oscar.

EXECUTE ROLE-PLAY (FOUR MIN):

	ALLY ROLE-PLAY ACTIONS	SKEPTIC ROLE-PLAY ACTIONS
1		The skeptic reads a version of the statement: "There is no such thing as white privilege."
2	Get the skeptic to say a bit more about their beliefs. Try something like: "That is an interesting point of view. Could you say more about what you think about that?"	
3		Skeptic expands by giving more belief statements.
4	Make an Ask: "Tell me some experience of yours that further confirms your view."	
5		Skeptic tells a story/anecdote.
6	Ally listens empathetically to make the skeptic feel truly heard.	Skeptic tunes in to how much they feel truly heard by the ally.
7	Ally creates a transition and brings up their own Connect story that relates to some piece of the embedded beliefs of the skeptic.	

DEBRIEFING THE ROLE-PLAY (FOUR MINUTES):

ALLY DISCUSSION QUESTIONS	SKEPTIC DISCUSSION QUESTIONS
How did your Listening Tip work? How did hearing the skeptic's story feel?	How much did your partner make you feel heard during when you told your story?
How did it feel to tell your Connect story?	How did it feel to play the role of the skeptic? What was difficult or easy about it?
What improvements would you like to make on your performance?	Any tips to help the ally sharpen their performance?

SWITCH ROLES AND REPEAT!

FULL RACE METHOD THROUGH THE EXPAND STEP

Choose which person is going play the role of the skeptic first. You will repeat the preparation steps from a few minutes ago.

EXECUTE ROLE-PLAY (SIX MIN):

	ALLY ROLE-PLAY ACTIONS	SKEPTIC ROLE-PLAY ACTIONS
1		The skeptic reads a version of the statement: "There is no such thing as white privilege."
2	Ally brings up statement, asks follow-up question to get skeptic to say more about their beliefs.	
3		Skeptic expands on beliefs.
4	Make an Ask to learn about an experience related to the skeptic's beliefs.	
5		Skeptic tells an experience related to the belief.
6	Ally listens empathetically enough to make the skeptic feel truly heard.	Skeptic tunes in to how much they feel truly heard by the ally.
7	Ally creates a transition and brings up their own Connect story that relates to some piece of the embedded beliefs of the skeptic.	
8	After letting the connection exist for a moment, ally creates a transition to signal they are going to tell a second story.	
9	Ally tells Expand story.	Skeptic listens empathetically.
10	Optional: Ally asks whether it is possible for two things that seem the opposite to both be true.	

SESSION FOUR
PREPARING TO SUSTAIN OUR JOURNEY

DEBRIEFING THE ROLE-PLAY (FIVE MINUTES):

ALLY DISCUSSION QUESTIONS	SKEPTIC DISCUSSION QUESTIONS
What did you do to get in/stay in a listening mode? What are some lessons you learned? How well did it work? How did hearing the skeptic's story feel?	How much did your partner make you feel heard as you shared your experience?
How did it feel to tell stories? How did your experience of telling the different stories compare.	How did it feel to play the role of the skeptic? What was difficult or easy about it?
What improvements would you like to make on your performance?	Any tips to help the ally sharpen their performance?

SWITCH ROLES AND REPEAT!

ALLY CONVERSATION TOOLKIT
(ACT) DISCUSSION LEADERS
GUIDE—COURSE #1

SESSION #4: PREPARING TO SUSTAIN OUR JOURNEY

LEARNING OBJECTIVES

- Reinforce norms for the group, such as Check-In and Triumphs and Trials.

- Build on the sense of community in the group.

- Learn ideas about conservative/liberal ideological differences and compare them to lived experiences.

- Engage in a discussion about the role that shame might be playing in ally work.

- Examine which racism-skeptics participants might think about engaging relatively soon.

- Ponder other allies to recruit to support your ongoing learning.

- To give people a chance to express their level of interest in being part of a second mini-course.

- (If time) Work on refining/creating Connect and Expand stories

PREPARATION BY THE LEADER FOR THE SESSION

- Read the section on conservatives and liberals—pp. 247-249, pp. 254-257.

- Complete the exercise on conservatives and liberals—pp. 250-251, pp. 256-257.

- Do some reflection on your own level of bias against conservatives and why the level is where it is.

- Engage the questions about shame on pp. 237-238.

- Engage the questions about choosing skeptics on pp. 240-242.

- If possible, prepare a second set of stories for unconscious bias and unearned racial advantage. Alternatively, review your existing stories and clarify improvements that you want to make in them.

- Bring a few extra copies of the Connect and Expand worksheets for unconscious bias and unearned privilege.

- Print out a copy of the Appendix 1 of this guide for each person.

PREPARATION BY THE PARTICIPANTS FOR THE SESSION

- Read commentary about conservatives and liberals— pp. 247-253, pp. 254-257.

- Review reading and reflection questions on shame—pp. 236-238.

- Review reading and reflection questions on choosing skeptics—pp. 239-242.

NOTE TO GROUP LEADER

This closing session of the Ally Fundamentals course has more processes than other sessions, and may take longer than two hours if you do every segment. Since this session represents the ending of a process, you may want to agree in advance to make the meeting longer than usual so that people can potentially say goodbye to each other. If this is not possible you may need to eliminate some of the processes suggested. There are two segments that are most suitable for abbreviating or skipping if you must adhere to the two-hour time frame.

First, there is a process for discussing the role that shame plays in interactions with other whites. This conversation is important but also emotionally risky. In addition, it takes some time to pursue. Guidance is provided below about how to point participants to the topic of shame while spending only a minimal amount of time on it during the session.

Second, there is a segment focused on refining anecdotes or developing new ones. Since the entire purpose of the course is to arm people with tools and anecdotes are a vital tool, having a process focused on augmenting your stockpile of anecdotes is an appropriate exercise for a session that represents graduation. However, as the leader, you should look at this segment as optional and only do it if you have time.

What should not be optional is having a moment where each member of the group reflects on and communicates their interest in reenlisting in more sessions as a learning community. This course is part of a social movement for using empathy-based strategies for dismantling racism. Giving participants a moment to decide if they want to reenlist in a formal ally learning process is a vital part of strengthening that movement.

In addition to the reenlist decision, you also need to leave time to do a closing ritual, which can vary in length depending on what you choose to do.

SEGMENT #1: CHECK-IN

Follow the sequence of the Check-In, including both the Getting Centered and the Triumphs and Trials, that was outlined earlier in this document.

SEGMENT #1.5: QUOTES AND EXCERPTS TO FOSTER COMMUNITY BUILDING (OPTIONAL)

See appendices for content for specific populations.

SEGMENT #2: UNDERSTANDING CONSERVATIVES AND LIBERALS

LEARNING OBJECTIVES

- Briefly review the way that moral foundations theory applies to conservatives and liberals.

- Discuss how conservatism and liberalism are broader concepts than political ideology.

- Examine the group's collective experiences of the way that conservative and liberal orientations live often differ in predictable ways.

- Examine and discuss biases that progressives often have about conservatives and how these biases can affect interactions.

SESSION FOUR
PREPARING TO SUSTAIN OUR JOURNEY

WHAT TO SAY TO OPEN THE CONVERSATION ABOUT CONSERVATIVE AND LIBERAL IDEOLOGY

Some of the new work we are going to do today focuses on increasing our understanding of the differences between conservatives and liberals, and how this might affect our ally work and communication with racism skeptics.

Not everyone can become familiar with each session's material before the session. Is there anybody who read the section about conservatives and liberals who would like to briefly summarize what they remember about how these groups differ when it comes to politics?

NOTE TO GROUP LEADERS

If someone is willing to summarize, let them do so. The key ideas that you want to get into the group are:

- Conservatives and liberals base their thinking about politics on different things.

- Many liberals have a bias against conservatives and want conservatives to not be conservative.

Some allies meld together their desire to diminish other people's racism skepticism and their desire to persuade people out of conservative approaches to politics. Melding these together can make it difficult to move conservatives about racism, because they rightly feel that their political ideology is being attacked.

DISCUSSION QUESTIONS

- Did anyone who read the commentary on pp. 247-253 and on pp. 254-257 have a reaction that it would be useful to discuss?

- In the commentary, the statement is made that it is important to believe in the possibility of there being anti-racist conservatives, even if you have never met one. Do you find yourself thinking that is important, wrong-headed, or something else?

WHAT TO SAY TO SHIFT THE FOCUS TO CONSERVATIVE AND LIBERAL ORIENTATIONS TO LIFE

As you may remember, there was commentary in the Workbook that asserted that we not only need to understand the differences between conservatives and liberals in politics, but that there are differences between folks beyond politics that we should pay attention to.

Let's start this conversation by doing an exercise in the Workbook; then we will talk about the issue.

NOTE TO THE GROUP LEADER

The following are instructions for engaging the group in the exercise about conservatives and liberals. Your goal is to have each person do the exercise for one or preferably two skeptics. At a precise moment, you will have each person reveal their results, so that the entire group can see the general trend in the group.

GROUP PROCESS

- Ask if people have done the conservative/liberal exercise on pp. 250-251. If some people have not done it, give everyone a chance to do the exercise. Review the instructions and give people guidance as necessary. Ideally, everyone will have "scores" for two racism skeptics in their world.

- Have everyone count the number of dimensions that skeptic #1 is to the right of them on the chart. Tell them to remember the number and be prepared to show it on their right hand on your count.

- For skeptic #2, have them count the number of dimensions that the skeptic's results are to the right of participants. They should be prepared to show this on their left hand on your count.

- Tell the group that we will all show our count and hold our hands out so that we can all see the similarities and differences between our counts.

- Tell the participants to privately answer the question about bias against conservatives, and tell them that the group will also discuss their answers to this question before the discussion is over.

- Have the group reveal the results for skeptics #1 and #2 at the same time.

- After the group can see the diversity of scores, have a discussion about the implications of the findings. In all likelihood, most people had four or five fingers showing, meaning that the skeptics the allies assessed were "more conservative" on a number of lifestyle dimensions beyond race and politics.

- The objective of the exercise is to allow the group to see the pattern of responses, but not have any implied judgment of people who vary from the pattern.

DISCUSSION QUESTIONS

- What do you think about the idea that racially skeptical views are linked to a more conservative approach to life generally? Does this seem relevant to the task of being a persuasive ally? Why or why not?

- What was your answer to the question about bias against conservatives? If you have some bias against conservatives, how does this manifest itself?

- Have you ever seen someone be affected by a bias against conservatives that they were not aware that they had?

- Do you have the impression that conservative people sometimes sense when you or other folks have some level of bias against them?

NOTE TO GROUP LEADERS

After the discussion feels reasonably complete, bring the conversation to a close, and tell them that you want to transition to a focus on the role of shame in how anti-racism allies interact with each other and with racism skeptics.

SEGMENT #3: HOW DOES SHAME AFFECT OUR ALLY WORK?

LEARNING OBJECTIVES

- To bring attention to the idea that it is common in the ally community for shame to play a notable role in people interactions with each other.

- To direct participants to the fact that the Workbook contains an exercise about shame they may choose to do on their own.

- If appropriate, to have a healthy conversation about shame when interacting with other whites.

NOTE TO GROUP LEADER

As mentioned earlier, you will need to make a decision about how to manage the group time during this session and to make sure you give sufficient time for the reenlist decision and for a closing ritual.

You should consider both time and emotional safety as you decide how much energy to spend on the issue of shame. The issue of shame can be difficult to discuss, by its very nature. Both before and during the meeting, take a moment of reflection about whether the level of candor and vulnerability in the group is sufficient to carry a conversation about shame.

INSTRUCTIONS IF THE GROUP LEADER THINKS A CONVERSATION ABOUT SHAME IS NOT SAFE

You may decide as the group leader that talking about this is needlessly risky or is simply less important than something else in this session. If so, it would still be useful to bring the group's attention briefly to the fact that the Workbook includes an important reflection exercise about shame that they can do privately and that can help their journey.

WHAT TO SAY TO INTRODUCE THE CONVERSATION ABOUT SHAME

One of the things we have to think about is the issue of shame and how it affects our interactions with skeptics and with other allies.

We are not going to focus on it as a group, but I recommend that you do the self-assessment exercise on pp. 236-238.

If you have another ally friend that you are close to emotionally, it may be helpful to discuss your results with them, and perhaps have them do the exercise so you can both talk about your results.

INSTRUCTIONS IF THE GROUP LEADER ASSESSES THAT A CONVERSATION ABOUT SHAME IS SAFE

WHAT TO SAY TO TRANSITION TO A CONVERSATION ABOUT SHAME

As the Workbook discusses on p. 235, the issue of guilt/shame is highly relevant for some allies and their response to both skeptics and other allies.

This project overall recognizes that many allies are affected by issues of shame regarding the quality and quantity of their contacts with people of color. While you might want to talk about that at some point, let's make sure that we spend some time focused on shame and our interaction with other allies and skeptics.

GROUP PROCESS

Encourage the group to answer the questions on pp. 236-238.

WHAT TO SAY

Let's go into the conversation with the understanding that shame might be one of those emotions that can affect some people a lot and others much less. As we discuss, let's try to give extra room in the conversation for those who say that they are affected to some notable extent.

GROUP PROCESS

Some or all of the following questions may be helpful to this discussion:

- Did you have any reaction to the Workbook commentary about the role of shame in interactions that allies have with each other and with skeptics?

- Were there ideas in the commentary that really resonated? Were there ideas that were strong clunkers for you?

- How did the process of answering those questions affect your perspective about shame?

- In what settings and with what type of people is that shame most relevant?

- Thinking about the ally community in general, what are settings with other whites in which shame/guilt is having the most impact?

- When did you first realize that shame/guilt affects your interaction with other white people? Were there signs that this was true that you ever suppressed from your awareness?

NOTE TO GROUP LEADERS

As the discussion continues, people may naturally refer to the instrument they completed before the discussion. If not, you might decide to encourage people to reveal their answers if they are comfortable. Be ready to model what you want by revealing your answers, especially for questions in which you think shame/guilt matters a great deal.

SEGMENT #4: CHOOSING PEOPLE TO PRIORITIZE FOR ENGAGEMENT

LEARNING OBJECTIVES

- Get each participant to review which skeptics and allies in their circle they might prioritize.

- Have a group conversation about choosing which skeptics to potentially focus on.

- Have a group conversation about choosing which allies to join your journey.

- If possible, refine participants' thinking about criteria for choosing skeptics.

PART 1: CHOOSING SKEPTICS TO PRIORITIZE
WHAT TO SAY

Thus far, much of our work has focused on how we might respond to racially problematic statements that come up in the general course of living.

As important as that is, it is also useful for us to think about whether there are people in our circle of influence that we might purposefully engage on issues related to racism. Even if we don't decide to immediately engage them, there is value in us thinking about the people in our lives that we might engage at some future point and to think about whom we want to focus on first, and whom we might save until we are more facile with these methods.

Let's take a minute to review pp. 239-242 of the Workbook. When you finish the reading, write down the skeptics you might consider engaging on p. 242.

SESSION FOUR
PREPARING TO SUSTAIN OUR JOURNEY

GROUP PROCESS
Each member of the group reads p. 239 and the top of p. 240.

DISCUSSION QUESTIONS

- What did you think of the criteria that the Workbook suggested as most useful in choosing skeptics to engage?

- Are there other criteria that you think are just as important?

- How difficult or easy was it to write down six skeptics on p. 240? Is there any significance to how easy or difficult this was?

NOTE TO GROUP LEADERS
There are anti-racism allies whose lives are so deeply entrenched in the "liberal bubble" that it is difficult for them to write down six skeptics they know. Some folks like this may be in your group. While you want to honor the reality everyone brings to the group, you may need to push people a bit because some folks immediately give up without challenging themselves to think about all of their extended network.

The following question may be helpful in pushing people: Who were the last two people who said racially problematic statements who were not strangers to you?

For the exercise, each person should come up with at least two skeptics, though having more than two will make the exercise more fruitful. Listing at least two people allows them to complete the exercise, which is on pp. 241-242 of the Workbook.

If a person feels strongly about additional criteria, encourage them to add the criteria to the table on p. 241. Have the participants articulate the new criteria so that the top of the scale represents factors that suggest choosing the person, and the bottom of the scale suggests not choosing the person.

GROUP PROCESS
Each person completes the table on p. 241, then uses the results to complete the table on p. 242 of the Workbook.

DISCUSSION QUESTIONS

- Were there any surprises or insights for you in doing the exercise?

- Did the prioritization order give you a different result than what you expected?

- Is there a part of you that wants to not follow the "guidance" of this exercise, and either prioritize or deprioritize people based on another part of your intuition? What do you think is driving that feeling?

PART 2: CHOOSING ALLIES TO SUPPORT YOUR JOURNEY
WHAT TO SAY TO INTRODUCE THE PROCESS OF THINKING ABOUT ALLIES WHO MIGHT SUPPORT US

Whether we continue as a group or not, at some point you will not be a part of a formal ally learning community. So it is valuable to think about which people in your circle can be a part of your informal support. This next segment is about considering the allies that you know who it might make sense to talk to about your ally journey so you can get support and perhaps give support to them.

To briefly explore possibilities in this regard, we are going to look at pp. 247-249 in the Workbook.

The first task is to think of six people in your circle of influence whom you think of as other allies. As you choose whom to write on this initial list, do not require that they be hardcore activists, although that is fine if they are. Rather, think of people that you have a good relationship with who would support your effort to become more effective at influencing racism skeptics, and might be interested in enhancing this ability within themselves.

If there are not six people like this in your circle, push yourself to list at least two. Write their names on p. 244 of the Workbook.

On p. 245, there is table that can help you reexamine this list with regard to four criteria. If there are some other criteria that you think are important for you in choosing other allies to ask for support, add them to the left of the names, and also rate the possible allies on the same scale from one to four.

GROUP PROCESS

When everyone is done, have a group conversation about these questions:

- Were there any surprises about which allies seemed most suitable for mutual support when you examined them through the criteria?

- How feasible would it be to make a conscious practice of talking about allyship with the people you think would be most suitable to support you?

SEGMENT #4.5: A POTENTIAL ALLY ROLE MODEL (OPTIONAL)

See appendices for content targeted to specific populations.

SEGMENT #5: AUGMENTING OUR TOOLKIT; REENLISTING; CLOSING RITUAL (OPTIONAL)

PART 1: AUGMENTING OUR STORIES (OPTIONAL)
LEARNING OBJECTIVE

- To have participants either polish some existing stories they already have or to add new stories to their toolkit.

NOTE TO GROUP LEADER

As noted, depending on how you manage the meeting, it may be impossible to do the preceding segments, to do the reenlist decision and closing rituals, and to execute this process. However, if you think you have time for everything, this process can be a great final learning exercise for the course, leaving people with an increased sense of confidence in their allyship.

WHAT TO SAY TO HELP EACH PERSON CHOOSE WHAT THEY WANT TO WORK ON

The project hopes that you have at least two to three Connect and Expand stories for unconscious bias, and two or three Connect and Expand stories for unearned racial advantage. The hope is that over time, these stories become part of your engagement arsenal and that you have gotten better and better at sharing them. In this course, we have practiced one Connect and Expand story for each of these topics.

You can choose to either develop an additional story set for one of these topics or you can work on refining your current stories. In a moment we will divide into pairs to work with someone who made the choice to either refine their anecdote arsenal or to expand it by working on a new story. Think about whether you want to develop a new pair of stories or revisit your existing stories.

If you choose to develop new stories you are going to go through the same process we did before, where we spend a few minutes writing, then doing a role-play. If you choose to sharpen an existing story, you will go directly to the role-play using your Connect and Expand stories, and get some feedback on your storytelling. Then you will do the role-play and story sequence a second time, hopefully integrating the feedback into an improved story.

Which do you want to do: sharpen your arsenal or expand it? Both are important, so you cannot make a bad choice.

GROUP PROCESS

- Survey each person on whether they want to work on unconscious bias or unearned racial advantage.

- After giving people a few minutes to choose, pair them with someone who made the same choice.

NOTE TO GROUP LEADER

Empower each pair to manage its time so that each person gets a chance to either refine their story or to work on a new story. For people who are working on a new story, refer to pp. 91-95 for unconscious bias or pp. 104-108 for unearned racial advantage. For people who have already filled out those pages in your Workbook, refer them to pp.167-168 for an extra worksheet for creating new stories.

PART 2: THE REENLIST DECISION
NOTE TO GROUP LEADER

Your objective is to give a gentle nudge to people in the direction of reenlisting in another Mini-Course where allies will meet to support each other and further enhance their effectiveness. However, you do not want to overly pressure people, or to give the impression that if they do not sign up. they will not be in a position to continue their journey toward becoming more effective allies.

WHAT TO SAY

I suspect that most of us recognize that although we have made some significant progress in our journey toward greater allyship, this is long-term work, perhaps lifelong work.

This was set up as a four-to-five-session Mini-Course so all of us could make an initial moderate commitment of time and energy, then decide whether staying in a learning community of allies was something we wanted to do right now.

The ACT project has given some guidance for two more mini-courses. If a person goes through all three Mini-Courses, they will have gone through the entire Workbook.

Next in the suggested sequence of mini-courses is a five-session sequence called Hot Topics. It will focus on the modules related to Race and Economics, Race and Crime, and Immigration. It will also cover some of the issues in Part 3 of the Workbook, such as racial anxiety and racial threat.

The other Mini-Course is Healing History and is composed of six sessions. The modules in that session focus on the idea that slavery was too long ago to think about, that no one is racist anymore, and that athletes and other people of color should stop protesting symbols of our heritage, such as the anthem. It will also deal with other concepts like racial backlash, denial, and grievance.

(At this point, hand out Appendix 2, which outlines the content of Mini-Courses 2 and 3).

The extensive guides for those mini-courses are still being created, but we already have an outline of the sequence of topics. Given what we have just been through, members of this group could go through another sequence if we wanted to.

Let's take the pulse of the group about our desire to continue meeting. Here is the question:

What is your level of interest in continuing to meet together as a learning community of allies working on how to increase our influence on others. Here is the scale:

» 1 represents definitely want to continue in a learning community.

» 2 is on the fence about continuing as a group.

» 3 is does not want to keep meeting as a group.

We will take a moment of silence so you can think about it. As you ponder the question, remember that if we continue meeting, we could change the structure, perhaps meeting more often, less often, meeting at a different place, or having a different leader. The people who want to continue can discuss all of those factors. The question on the table is our level of interest in continuing to meet, even if we change the conditions.

On a count of three, let's reveal our number.

NOTE TO GROUP LEADER

- If most of the group wants to keep meeting, focus the conversation on how to make this happen.

- If most of the group does not want to meet, go around the group to find out why that is. Please take notes on the answers and later submit these answers to ACT. This is important feedback for the project.

- If there is significant variation within the group, make note of who wants to continue, and solicit a commitment to have a brief meeting before you depart about how the group will continue. Only after the group makes a plan to plot their next steps should you give some room for those who want to stop to express why. This sequence is important so that the people who want to continue are not dissuaded from hearing the motivations of those who want to stop.

- When those who want to stop express their reasons why, please take notes of these reasons and later submit them to ACT.

PART 3: CLOSING THE MEETING AND THE MINI-COURSE
NOTE TO GROUP LEADER

Even if everyone in the group wants to reenlist, it is useful to do a closing process to recognize that the group has completed an important journey. Try to do a closing ritual that is suitable to the moment, which includes the duration of the meeting thus far, the level of positive connectivity in the group, and the likelihood of members of the group meeting again.

Here are some options for a closing process:
- **One word (super short)**—everyone say one word expressing how they feel as this process ends.

- **One phrase (short)**—everyone say one short phrase expressing how they feel.

- **Statement of gratitude or takeaway (medium-length)**—every person makes one statement of appreciation/gratitude or a thing they will take away from this experience.

- **Looking back and forward (long)**—each person says one takeaway from the process and one thing they will do in the future as a result of having been through the process.

Finally: Please take a closing picture and send it to ACT. If possible, take one regular picture and one "funny face/strike a pose" picture.

APPENDIX 1: REFINING YOUR STORY – A FOUR-ROUND PROCESS

Choose which person is going to play the ally and who will be the skeptic in Round 1.

ROUND 1

1. The skeptic makes a racially problematic statement related to the topic the ally is working on.

2. The ally asks a follow-up question, nudging the skeptic to say more about their beliefs.

3. The skeptic briefly expounds on their beliefs.

4. The ally asks the skeptic to share an experience that animates the skeptic's beliefs (the Ask step).

5. The skeptic tells an experience that is designed to be the kind of anecdote that a skeptic might tell to justify their previously stated belief.

6. The ally listens empathetically, with the intention of making the skeptic feel heard.

7. The ally tells a Connect story that is designed to make the skeptic feel that on some level, the ally and the skeptic share a common perspective on something related to the core topic (the Connect step).

8. The skeptic pays attention to the level of impact of the ally's Connect story, especially how much the story helps create an emotional connection.

9. The ally pauses to let the connection between the people be felt.

10. The Ally creates a transition, then tells an Expand story that invites the skeptic to consider the reality of unconscious bias or unearned racial advantage (the Expand step).

11. The skeptic pays attention to the effectiveness of the ally's Expand story, especially how much the story conveys the sense that many reasonable white people might come to the same conclusion about unconscious bias or unearned racial advantage.

DEBRIEF QUESTIONS
FOR THE SKEPTIC

- How much did the ally make you feel heard while you told your story? Is there anything they might have done to enhance your sense of being heard?

- How much did the Connect story make you feel connected to the ally? What would have been some possible tweaks to make the story more effective?

- To what extent did the Expand story make you feel like this could have happened to you, or that you might have come to the same conclusion?

FOR THE ALLY

- Can you see any things you might have done to make the skeptic feel more heard?

- What, if any, possible improvements to your stories do you see?

- If there were some choices you debated about in telling your story, share those choices with the skeptic and get their feedback.

Before switching roles, the ally should write down at least two concrete changes they plan to make when doing this again.

ROUND 2
Switch roles, repeat the same process as above.

ROUND 3
Switch roles again, with the first ally making the changes they wrote down as well as other lessons they might have learned from serving as the skeptic in Round 2.

ROUND 4
Switch roles again, integrating lessons from all previous rounds.

APPENDICES

Session 1	Session 2	Session 3	Session 4	Session 5
Check-In	Check-In	Check-In	Check-In	Check-In
Refresher and Update	Racial Threat, p. 209	Racial Backlashes, p. 213	Module 7: Immigration, p. 149	Black Lives Matter (see website)
Reflections and Accomplishments	Module 6: No one racist any more, p. 139 (Work on Connect and Expand stories)	Making Asks, including the Apologetic Non-Apology (see website)	Past experience of convincing or being convinced, p. 230	Check-In about recruiting to grow the ally movement
Refining Your Stories		Recruiting other allies to make this journey	Institutional/ Structural racism, p. 219	Institutional changes we can influence
				How do we take our messages to grow the ally movement?

APPENDIX 2: GUIDE FOR MINI-COURSES 2 AND 3

If your group has gone through Mini-Course 1, the group should have a sense of the next processes it needs to learning. As a result, the Guide provides an overall map through the workbook instead of detailed instructions. If you need more guidance, please contact the project at www. allyconversationtoolkit.com.

MINI-COURSE 2: HOT TOPICS

Session 1	Session 2	Session 3	Session 4	Session 5
Check-In	Check-In	Check-In	Check-In	Check-In
Ground Rules	Module 3: Race & Economics, p. 112	Othering, p. 183	Module 5: Race and Law Enforcement, p.130	Module 8: Patriotism and Protests, p. 157
Ally Priorities Tool, p. 3	Going Deeper, p. 116	Refining our toolkit for unearned racial advantage, p. 100	Going Deeper, p. 133	Shame, p. 235
Making Asks (see website)	Racial Anxiety, p. 199		Attribution Error, p. 195	Ally Assessment Tool, p. 44
Improving our stories			Choosing Skeptics, p. 238	Reenlist decision

APPENDIX 3: GUIDE TO GROUP-SPECIFIC MATERIALS

The White Ally Toolkit Workbook and this Discussion Guide are intended to be of useful to any group of anti-racism allies who want to meet regularly to support each other in working through the exercises and learning the methods laid out in the White Ally Toolkit Workbook. As discussed, this Discussion Guide has given detailed instructions about Mini-Course 1, which is four (or five) sessions. Appendix 1 provides less detailed guidance about how a group might migrate through the rest of the Workbook. The presumption is that a group that has experienced Mini-Course 1 does not need detailed small group process instruction. Thus, the descriptions of Mini-Courses 2 and 3 focus on the sequence of topics that should be focused on.

The Workbook and the Discussion Guide were written with the assumption is that these anti-racism allies will not necessarily have any particular common identity or professional background. However, the Ally Conversation Toolkit project encourages the formation of learning groups will consist of people with a common connection to a community, an institution, a profession or some other common thread. Such groups can provide extra encouragement, motivation, and support to allies by helping them see the connection between their community identity and their journey as allies trying to dismantle racism. The purpose of these appendices is to provide additional content that a community-specific discussion group leader can use in these cases.

The material in these appendences is based on the idea that when an anti-racism learning group has a common identity, the group leader can take specific steps to reinforce the course content and solidify the coherence of the group. Specifically, the group leader can take a moment or two during each session to focus on the link between the session content and the group members' sense of identity as members of that community.

As the reader has seen, each session outline delineates two specific moments – Segments 1.5 and Segment 4.5 - that might be appropriate for this strategy of connecting group identity to the work at hand. Of course, group leaders can use their own discretion about whether, when, and how to create such moments of community building.

The appendices that follow provide useful material for such moments. Although each appendix is not precisely same, they are generally structured to provide the following content for each session:

The appendices provide supplemental material that gives leaders material for such small moments during each session. For each session, the appendices may provide:

- One to three short inspirational quotations that relate to the theme of the Session or anti-racist work in general

- Short biographical sketches of people who took concrete actions to counter systems of oppression

- One to two paragraph excerpts that illustrate the way that anti-oppression is described by a source that the specific community likely respects

The guide suggests that the leaders highlight the theme after the Check-In, read the quotations, and briefly review the excerpts. It also suggests that toward the end of the session, the leader move group attention to the role model.

Group leaders can use this additional material in a wide variety of ways. Some possible options for using this material:

- Read aloud the inspirational quotations that emphasize the theme of the session, have a moment of silent reflection, then have a short discussion about the theme.

- Review the excerpts, discuss whether the excerpt reflects a sentiment that the community should rally around.

- Have each person silently read the ally role model description, then discuss any implications for the group's journey toward more effective allyship.

APPENDICES

Appendix 4 provides material that can be used for a group of allies that may have no specific community connection. Since there is no overarching institution, there are no institutional excerpts in this appendix. There are several quotations, including a few from sources that might be considered surprising.

Appendix 5 is designed to be of use to a group that might include social workers and mental health professionals, educators, and community organizers. It was put together by Angela Kremer, of Cascadia Health, Portland, OR.

Appendix 6 provides materials that might be useful for a group of anti-racism allies who are linked by their connection to the fields of facilitation, mediation, and/or conflict resolution. Assistance in its compilation was provided by Tim Bonneman of Intellitics (www.intellitics.com).

Appendix 7 provides materials that might be useful for anti-racism allies who think of themselves as conservative Christians. It was put together by Christian blogger and World News Group commentator Mary Butler Coleman (www.thestudiousmom.com).

The supplemental material is organized, broadly speaking, to be reinforcing of the session content or background imperative for allies to make related to the session. These imperatives are:

- Session 1: Making a Strong Commitment
- Session 2: Maintaining Humility and Reflection
- Session 3: Fighting Unfairness
- Session 4: Sustaining the Ally Journey

Appendix 8 provides potential role models that might be useful for anti-racism allies who think of themselves as progressive and/or liberal Christians.

APPENDIX 4: SUPPLEMENTAL MATERIAL FOR GROUPS WITH NO SPECIFIC CONNECTION

Commitment is what transforms a promise into a reality. — Abraham Lincoln

Commitment means staying loyal to what you said you were going to do long after the mood you said it in has left you. — Anonymous

No problem of human making is too great to be overcome by human ingenuity, human energy, and the untiring hope of the human spirit. — George H.W. Bush

Unless a commitment is made there are only promises and hopes, but no plans. — Peter Drucker

ALLY ROLE MODEL: VIOLA LIUZZO

Viola Luizzo's activation as an anti-racism ally began with a chance conversation in a grocery store line with Sarah Evans, a black woman. Eventually, Sarah woked for Viola as a housekeeper, and they developed a close friendship. Through the insights into Sarah's life, Viola became aware of the daily indignities and structural barriers that defined the American color line at the time.

Viola's increasing awareness of societal obstacles pushed her to become increasingly active in efforts for racial equality. Liuzzo so passionately believed in the fight for civil rights that she helped organize Detroit protests and attended civil rights conferences. She also was one of the few white members of the Detroit chapter of the NAACP.

After hearing Rev. Dr. Martin Luther King, Jr. call for people of all faiths to come and help the struggle for voting rights in Alabama, she decided to travel there to support the movement. This call prompted Viola to leave her children in the care of family and friends and travel to the deep South.

While shuttling other volunteers as part of an organizing by the Southern Christian Leadership Conference, Viola was accosted by KKK members who noticed that her passenger was black. After following her for some time, the Klansmen shot at the car, missing her passenger but killing her instantly. Her funeral was attended by both civil rights and political luminaries such as Martin Luther King, as well as leaders of national labor unions. Two weeks after her death, a cross was burned on her front lawn.

SESSION 2 THEME: HUMILITY/REFLECTION

Nothing is so difficult as not deceiving oneself. — Ludwig Wittgenstein

It is easier to fight for one's principles than to live up to them. — Alfred Adler

It's on the strength of observation and reflection that one finds a way. So we must dig and delve unceasingly. — Claude Monet

O, happy the soul that saw its own faults. – Rumi

Everyone thinks of changing the world, but no one thinks of changing himself. — Leo Tolstoy

ALLY ROLE MODEL: WILL CAMPBELL
Will Campbell was an author, pastor, and civil rights activist. In 1957, while working for the National Council of Churches, Campbell participated in two notable events of the Civil Rights Movement: He was one of four people who escorted the black students who integrated the Little Rock, Arkansas public schools; He was the only white person present at the founding of the Southern Christian Leadership Conference.

Campbell was one of the four people who escorted the black students who integrated the Little Rock, Ark., public schools in 1957. In 1961, he helped "Freedom Riders" of the Congress of Racial Equality and the Student Non-Violent Coordinating Committee to integrate interstate bus travel, despite white mob violence, in Alabama.

He appealed to Southern Christian churches to end their own segregation and fight discrimination, rather than remain silent. Campbell eventually left organized religion, though he remained firmly Christian.

Bernard Lafayette, a civil rights leader said, "When we had the sit-ins, Will would show up. We knew there was somebody who cared and was concerned about what happened to us. He was reminding us that there were some white people who believed in what we were doing."

SESSION 3 THEME: UNFAIRNESS

We must challenge a system that simply shuffles children through grade to grade, without determining whether they can read, write, and add and subtract. It's a system — see, I like to call it this: We need to challenge the soft bigotry of low expectations. If you have low expectations, you're going to get lousy results. We must not tolerate a system that gives up on people. — George W. Bush

Yet, Americans often see race first and the individual second. That means each individual assumes all the costs of racial stereotypes with none of the benefits of American individuality. As long as any white American looks at black Americans and associates color with violence, sloth, or sexual license, then all black Americans carry the burden of some black Americans. That is unfair. As long as any black American looks at white Americans and associates color with oppression, paternalism, and dominance all white Americans wear the racist exploiter label of some white Americans. That is unfair. — Bill Bradley

APPENDICES

Racism and inequality are likened to a fungus which grows in dark places and is all the more poisonous because one cannot see it. — Michael R. French

ALLY ROLE MODEL: RAMSAY CLARK

Ramsay Clark occupied senior positions in the Justice Department of the Kennedy and Johnson administrations. In March of 1967, he was sworn in as the attorney general. This promotion reflected a number of achievements, including one year when he returned $200,000 to the treasury because his division fulfilled its mandates while implementing efficiency measures.

Though having a soft-spoken demeanor, Clark was a fierce advocate for civil rights and used his position in service of allyship on many occasions. Some of the more notable examples include when he:

- supervised the federal presence at the University of Mississippi during the week following the admission of James Meredith;

- surveyed all school districts in the South desegregating under court order (1963);

- supervised federal enforcement of the court order protecting the Selma-to-Montgomery marches;

- headed the Presidential task force to Watts following the disturbances in 1968.

- supervised the drafting and executive role in passage of the Voting Rights Act of 1965 and Civil Rights Act of 1968

Clark was a key player in the department's civil rights activities, intimately involved with desegregation efforts at the Universities of Mississippi and Alabama, with the federal government's involvement in the freedom rides, the lunch counter sit-ins, and the March to Selma and, later in the Johnson administration, working with Martin Luther King, Jr. and other civil rights leaders.

Success may require a lot of days. But progress only requires one. — T. Jay Taylor

Part of being optimistic is keeping one's head pointed toward the sun, one's feet moving forward. — Nelson Mandela

The people who move forward and overcome their fears do not have some special powers or a magic pill they take; they just have more practice in facing their fears. — Dave Anderson

Do the one thing you think you cannot do. Fail at it. Try again. Do better the second time. The only people who never tumble are those who never mount the high wire. — Oprah Winfrey

ALLY ROLE MODEL: ELEANOR ROOSEVELT

Eleanor Roosevelt was the First Lady of the United States from 1933 until 1944. Some have argued that she played a major role in the creating of the modern First Lady role, because of her outspokenness on a variety of social issues of the day. She was particularly known for her energetic advocacy of changing existent norms of racial segregation and degradation.

Some of her actions were largely symbolic but still had significant impact because of the prominence of her position. For example, she broke with White House tradition by inviting hundreds of African American guests to the White House. In another example, when the black singer Marian Anderson was denied the use of Washington's Constitution Hall by the Daughters of the American Revolution in 1939, Eleanor resigned from the group in protest and helped arrange another concert on the steps of the Lincoln Memorial.

Her advocacy for racial equality also applied to matters that were not symbolic. Eleanor became one of the only voices in the Roosevelt White House insisting that benefits be equally extended to Americans of all races. In 1934, she lobbied behind the scenes for the 1934 Costigan-Wagner Bill to

APPENDICES

make lynching a federal crime. Following the Japanese attack on Pearl Harbor December 7, 1941, Roosevelt spoke out against Japanese-American prejudice, warning against the "great hysteria against minority groups". She also privately opposed her husband's executive order that required Japanese-Americans in many areas of the U.S. to enter internment camps.

Her advocacy for the cause of racial inclusion was noticed across the racial spectrum. When race riots broke out in Detroit in June 1943, critics in both the North and South wrote that Eleanor Roosevelt was to blame. At the same time, she grew so popular among African Americans, previously a reliable Republican voting bloc, that they became a consistent base of support for the Democratic Party.

APPENDIX 5: SUPPLEMENTAL MATERIAL FOR GROUPS LINKED TO EDUCATION, SOCIAL WORK, AND COMMUNITY ORGANIZING

SESSION 1 THEME: COMMITMENT

We need imagination and integrity, courage and a high heart. We need to fan the spark of conviction, which may again inspire the world as we did with our new idea of the dignity and the worth of free men. But first we must learn to cast out fear. People who "view with alarm" never build anything.

One thing I believe profoundly: We make our own history. The course of history is directed by the choices we make and our choices grow out of the ideas, the beliefs, the values, the dreams of the people. It is not so much the powerful leaders that determine our destiny as the much more powerful influence of the combined voice of the people themselves.
— Eleanor Roosevelt, First Lady of the United States

Community action is a core mission of activism in counseling and psychology, and the ally role is often viewed as integral to this work...During the training at a multicultural internship site, we noticed the limitations of naming white trainees as "allies" in anti-racist clinical practice. We discussed the importance of white counselors and psychologists becoming central to multicultural work instead of on the sidelines, as people with cultural identities implicated in and affected by racism. White ally activism has been a focus of study we found little research on that critically evaluated this position.....We found that the ally role doesn't account for the role of intersectionality...which generally refers to the notion that an individual embodies multiple social identities, some of which may be oppressed or privileged, and intersect to uniquely shape one's experience.

The power status of the ally [is] "working to end the system of oppression that gives them greater privilege and power based upon their social group membership." [In addition, allies should] "speak up against systems of oppression, and to challenge other whites to do the same.   Yet another model of ally identification involves a sense of political solidarity through the agreement of a need for social change between a both group and its members. In general, the role of the ally is to spread awareness among a dominant group and support the activism of members of a marginalized group.

— Evaluating the Ally Role: Contributions, Limitations, and the Activist Position in Counseling and Psychology from Journal for Social Action in Counseling and Psychologoy Vo. 8, No. 1, Summer 2016, by Lauren Mizock, PhD, and Konjit V. P., PhD

ALLY ROLE MODEL: LILLIAN WALD

Lillian Wald was a social reformer and public health advocate. She is notable for a number of accomplishments in the field of social work/ public health. She founded one the of the first settlement houses serving immigrants in New York city — the Henry Street Settlement — which eventually became Visiting Nurse Service of New York. This organization is sometimes referred to as the first public health center. She persuaded Columbia University to appoint the first professor of nursing at a U.S. college or university. She persuaded President Theodore Roosevelt to create a Federal Children's Bureau to protect children from abusive child labor. She is often credited with coining the term, "public health nurse" to describe nurses whose work is integrated into the public community.

In addition to her general contributions to the social work/public health professions, she was also a social justice activist in a number of ways that demonstrated allyship. She eschewed the common practice of segregated classrooms, and insisted that Henry Settlement House provide classes on health to everyone in an integrated setting. Most significantly, she is one of the few white founding members of the NAACP, which was created in 1909. The founding convention of the organization -- a group that emerged out of the controversial Niagara Movement — took place at Henry Settlement House, due to her advocacy with funders and other key white decision-makers.

SESSION 2 THEME: HUMILITY AND REFLECTION

We often think of peace as the absence of war; that if the powerful countries would reduce their arsenals, we could have peace. But if we look deeply into the weapons, we see our own minds - our prejudices, fears, and ignorance. Even if we transported all the bombs to the moon, the roots of war and the reasons for bombs would still be here, in our hearts and minds, and sooner or later we would make new bombs. Seek to become more aware of what causes anger and separation, and what overcomes them. Root out the violence in your life, and learn to live compassionately and mindfully. — Thich Nhat Hanh, monk and peace activist

Social work schools are increasingly incorporating courses on racism into the curriculum or revising existing ones. The University of Washington offers the course "Poverty and Inequality: An Analysis of Poverty and Inequality in the United States," including socioeconomic dimensions of stratification, including race, ethnicity, class, gender, immigration status, disability, age, sexual orientation, and family structure. Another course is "Social Work for Social Justice: Developing a Personal-Professional Stance." It uses critically self-reflective, experiential, and dialogue learning processes to engage students to explore personal meaning systems and narratives in the context of professional values of social justice, multiculturalism, empowerment, and globalization. — The New Social Worker: The Social Work Careers Magazine, Barbara Trainin Blank, Racism: the Challenge for Social Workers

APPENDICES

In 1986, Dr. Peggy McIntosh founded the National SEED Project on Inclusive Curriculum (Seeking Educational Equity and Diversity). SEED's mission is to transform classrooms in to climates that are multicultural, gender-fair, and inclusive of all students regardless of their backgrounds. The primary innovation of SEED is to modify classrooms based on collective wisdom embedded in the direct testimonies of teachers, parents, and communities. SEED has trained 2,200 K-16 teachers in forty states and fourteen countries. As a result, millions of students have been impacted by SEED's inclusive participatory approaches.

Despite the broad impact and lasting impact of SEED, Dr. McIntosh might be most well known for her 1989 article "White Privilege: Unpacking the Invisible Knapsack". This work is considered a pioneering contribution in the effort to putting the dimension of privilege into discussions of power, gender, race, class and sexuality in the United States. McIntosh used the metaphor of white privilege as "an invisible weightless knapsack of special provisions, assurances, tools, maps, guides, codebooks, passports, visas, clothes, compass, emergency gear, and blank checks." In the article, McIntosh lists scores of her own everyday advantages, such as "I can be sure that my children will be given curricular materials that testify to the existence of their race"; and "If a traffic cop pulls me over or if the IRS audits my tax return, I can be sure I haven't been singled out because of my race." It is arguable that one primary reason that the term white privilege has a place in popular culture is because of Dr. McIntosh's work.

SESSION 3 THEME: UNFAIRNESS

We are still conditioning people in this country and, indeed, all over the globe, to the myth of white superiority. We are constantly being told that we don't have racism in this country anymore, but most of the people who are saying that are white. White people think it isn't happening because it isn't happening to them. — Jane Elliot, equity trainer

Social workers pursue social change, particularly with and on behalf of vulnerable and oppressed individuals and groups of people. Social workers' social change efforts are focused primarily on issues of poverty, unemployment, discrimination, and other forms of social injustice. These activities seek to promote sensitivity to and knowledge about oppression and cultural and ethnic diversity. Social workers strive to ensure access to needed information, services, and resources; equality of opportunity; and meaningful participation in decision making for all people. – Social Work Education: From the University of St. Catherine/St. Thomas School of Social Work online magazine about social work alumnae and racism.

ALLY ROLE MODEL: JANE ELLIOTT

On the day after Martin Luther King, Jr. was assassinated, a conversation in the class of third grade teacher Jane Elliott culminated with the students saying they would like to find out what discrimination felt like. She divided the all-white classroom into two groups based on eye color. She explained that one group was superior to the others, and proceeded to treat them accordingly. A few days later, she informed the class that she had been misinformed about which group was superior. In both phases of the experiment, the academic and behavioral performance of the less-esteemed group worsened significantly.

When the experiment was over, Elliott instructed the students to write an essay about their experience. Some of these letters were published in the local newspaper; After the Associated Press picked up the story, Elliott become national story very quickly.; she appeared on the Johnny Carson Show, among other national media outlets. In 1970, she conducted the Blue Eyes Brown Eyes exercise at the White House for a conference of educators. A documentary film was done about her exercise and its affect on the participants decades later.

Although her innovative work was lauded by many, she was also despised by a substantial portion of the public. After her appearance in national media, only one of her fellow teachers continued to speak to her. In her hometown of Riceville Indiana, she was called that "nigger lover" on more than one occasion. During workshops, she has been struck, had a knife pulled on her, and has been threatened with being shot.

At 85, Elliott still travels the county doing training. Her exercise is often considered to be the forerunner to the entire field of diversity training.

SESSION 4 THEME: PERSISTENCE

"Every artist, every scientist, must decide now where he stands. He has no alternative. There is no standing above the conflict on Olympian heights. There are no impartial observers. Through the destruction, in certain countries, of the greatest of man's literary heritage, through the propagation of false ideas of racial and national superiority, the artist, the scientist, the writer is challenged. The struggle invades the formerly cloistered halls of our universities and other seats of learning. The battlefront is everywhere. There is no sheltered rear." And I saw, too, that the struggle for Negro rights was an inseparable part of the anti-fascist struggle and I said: "The artist must elect to fight for Freedom or for Slavery. I have made my choice. I had no alternative." — Paul Robeson, artist, civil rights activist

Social workers treat each person in a caring and respectful fashion, mindful of individual differences and cultural and ethnic diversity. Social workers promote clients' socially responsible self-determination. Social workers seek to enhance clients' capacity and opportunity to change and to address their own needs. Social workers are cognizant of their dual responsibility to clients and to the broader society. They seek to resolve conflicts between clients' interests and the broader society's interests in a socially responsible manner consistent with the values, ethical principles, and ethical standards of the profession. — The Code of Ethics National Association of Social Workers

ALLY ROLE MODEL: PAUL WELLSTONE

Senator Paul Wellstone spent much of his career before electoral politics as a professor in political science at Carleton College. Though he was a college professor, much of his time was spent in activist causes that reflected his deepest love, which was community organizing. He founded the Organization for a Better Rice County, a group consisting mainly of single parents on welfare. The organization advocated for public housing, affordable health care, improved public education, free school lunches, and a publicly funded day care center.

Senator Wellstone said of himself, "I want to be known as a civil rights senator." As a politician, there were a number of examples of his demonstrating racial allyship that was considered very disruptive and somewhat risky at the time.

During his first electoral campaign, for state auditor in 1982, part of his platform was advocacy for divestment of state funds from corporations who did business with the apartheid regime in South Africa.

When he arrived at the senate in 1990, he infuriated many of his colleagues in this chamber — which operated via a network of chummy relationships — by openly denouncing the "racist politics" of Senator Jesse Helms.

In 1991, he joined and addressed 3,000 protestors outside a World Series game between the Minnesota Twins and the Atlanta Braves. The protestors were drawing attention to the name of the Atlanta team as well as the Tomahawk Chop gesture that attempted to rally their fans.

His allyship did not go unrecognized. Native American activist Winona LaDuke described Wellstone, before his death in a plane crash in 2002, as a "champion of the vast majority of our issues."

APPENDIX 6: SUPPLEMENTAL MATERIAL FOR GROUPS LINKED TO CONFLICT RESOLUTION, FACILITATION, AND MEDIATION

SESSION 1 THEME: COMMITMENT

One of the hardest things in life to learn are which bridges to cross and which bridges to burn. — Oprah Winfrey

If you fear making anyone mad, then you ultimately probe for the lowest common denominator of human achievement. — Jimmy Carter

A leader does not deserve the name unless he is willing occasionally to stand alone. — Henry Kissinger

ALLY ROLE MODEL: MARTHA MCCOY

Martha McCoy joined the Everyday Democracy organization (previously called the Study Circles Resource Center) in 1991 as a program associate. In 1995, she became the executive director. She has used her position of influence to refine the organization's focus from dialogue on a wide variety of issues to making ED into a national leader in prompting the use of a racial equity lens as a key social change innovation.

Her focus on promoting racial equity has manifested itself within her organization as well. Early in her tenure as executive director, she recognized that there were a number of aspects of the organization that would likely limit its ability to become a leader in the field of racial equity. For starters, the staff and board tended to be 25% and 10% nonwhite respectively. In addition, non-whites also had shorter tenures within the organization.

Largely as part of its commitment to diversify the organization's staff and board, Martha persuaded the board to move the headquarters of the organization from rural Pomfret, Connecticut so that it could diversify its talent pool of the board and staff. In order to consciously shift its culture away from purely Eurocentric norms, Martha instituted a process of organization-wide training on how to apply a racial equity lens to all aspects of ED.

These efforts were effortful, complex, and were not without intense opposition. At one point, the Board and Martha faced the public relations and legal challenges of a court case challenging its efforts to make an equity lens a core part of its work. Nevertheless, Martha persisted in her commitment to organizational change. Currently, the organization is based in Hartford, and its staff is 75% people of color. In addition, the number of nonwhite members of the board has increased five-fold.

SESSION 2 THEME: HUMILITY/REFLECTION

A great many people think they are thinking when they are merely rearranging their prejudices. – David Bohm

It's probably unfair to expect the world at large, or even most people, to see us for all we are. It is essential, however, that we see ourselves for all we are. – Victoria Moran

A lot of people want to change the world, but only a few people want to change themselves. When it comes to the issue of race in America, we have to do both. – Bill Bradley

As individuals and as professionals, we must be continually mindful of how we exercise our power as Facilitators when helping groups achieve their desired outcomes. Awareness is the first step towards insight. Consideration and reflection are in the interests of each of us, our profession as a whole, and in the interests of those we serve.

APPENDICES

The value of a professional Code of Ethics is limited to the consideration and reflection we give to the Code and how we each apply it in the circumstances of our professional practice. As Facilitators, we are architects of trust. We owe it to our clients to act with an informed appreciation of the ethical issues and competencies needed to help groups build consensus and produce meaningful outcomes.
— Becoming a Reflective Practitioner: The Reflective Ethical Facilitator's Guide, Kimberley Bain, BGC Publishing, Ottawa CN, September 2014

ALLY ROLE MODEL: FRANK DUKES

For fifteen years, Dr. Frank Dukes has been the Director of the Institute for Environmental Negotiation (IEN) at the University of Virginia. The Institute focuses on helping individuals, communities, and public agencies find just solutions related to the vital problem of environmental sustainability. A great portion of his work focuses on projects involving environment and land use, community development, health, and education at the local, state, and federal levels.

In addition to his work on environmental issues, Dr. Dukes has spent a significant amount of his energy on the causes of racial equity and reconciliation. Professor Dukes is heavily involved in the "Transforming Community Spaces" project, which focuses on providing support for communities addressing deep differences over monuments, memorials, and other public representations of racial history. His interest in this is also illustrated by his work with the Charlottesville Commission on Race, Memorials, and Public Spaces. In this project, Professor Dukes worked to offer recommendations for how Charlottesville may tell more complete narratives in these public spaces so that they become less divisive as well as more historically accurate.

Professor Dukes also founded the University & Community Action for Racial Equity (UCARE), which addresses head-on the University's legacy of slavery, segregation, and its impact on the wider community. In recognition of his community service on this project and others, he received UVA's 2016 John T. Casteen III Diversity-Equity-Inclusion Leadership Award this year for dedicating a significant part of their careers to making those three words – "diversity," "equity" and "inclusion" –- a reality on Grounds, improving the climate for all.

SESSION 3 THEME: UNFAIRNESS

Today, cultural and legal changes mean that individuals expect and demand a voice in decisions that affect their lives and often they have the power to undermine those decisions if they aren't allowed their voice. – Daniel Yankelovich

We strive to engender an environment of respect and safety where all participants trust that they can speak freely and where individual boundaries are honoured. We use our skills, knowledge, tools, and wisdom to elicit and honour the perspectives of all.

We seek to have all relevant stakeholders represented and involved. We promote equitable relationships among the participants and facilitator and ensure that all participants have an opportunity to examine and share their thoughts and feelings. We use a variety of methods to enable the group to access the natural gifts, talents and life experiences of each member. – Professional Code of Ethics, International Association of Facilitators

COMMUNITY ROLE MODEL: DR. JIM LAUE
Dr. Jim Laue is widely considered a luminary in the conflict resolution field. He co-founded and chaired the National Peace Academy Campaign in 1976, which eventually evolved into the US Institute for Peace and the National Peace Institute Foundation, which Jim also chaired in the 1980s. He was also the first person to be appointed to an endowed chair in the field of conflict resolution, a position he held at George Mason University. At other points in his illustrious career, he held faculty positions at Washington University in St. Louis and at Harvard.

APPENDICES

As a graduate student, Laue was deeply involved in the civil rights movement. He was heavily involved with the SLCL and SNCC and joined others putting themselves at risk during the lunch counter sit-ins and church kneel-ins. At the time, these actions to fight the segregation that was common were considered extremely provocative and often induced mob violence against the protestors. His involvement in the civil rights movement was central to his doctoral dissertation: Direct Action and Desegregation - Toward a theory of the Rationalization of Protest.

In 1965, he joined the Community Relations Service, a fledging government agency that attempted to quell social conflict through dialogue and peacebuilding efforts. As part of his work with CRS, he came to Memphis in 1968 to help resolve the Sanitation Workers Strike and to lend support to Dr. King and his cause. He was one of only two white guests saying at the Lorraine Hotel on the day Dr. King was murdered and can be seen on some of the photographs after the shooting.

SESSION 4 THEME: PERSISTENCE

My faith demands — this is not optional — my faith demands that I do whatever I can, wherever I can, whenever I can, for as long as I can with whatever I have to try to make a difference. — Jimmy Carter

The greatest glory in living is not in falling, but in rising every time we fall. — Nelson Mandela

Surround yourself only with people who are going to take you higher. — Oprah Winfrey

The American Arbitration Association is the global leader in conflict management with core values of integrity and service. Our integrity demands impartial and fair treatment of all people with whom we come in contact, regardless of gender, race, ethnicity, age, religion, sexual orientation, or other characterization. Our conflict management services put into

practice our goal for the resolution of disputes between parties with different perspectives, experiences, and backgrounds.
— American Arbitration Association

COMMUNITY ROLE MODEL: DICK SALEM

Early in his career, Dick Salem served as the director of the Small Business Administration under President Johnson, and spent several years contributing to the administration's War on Poverty. This experience heightened his interest in the way that racial issues affected disputes. He subsequently became the Midwest Director of the Community Relations Service. From that platform, he was involved in several high profile disputes that were highly racialized.

For example, he played a key role in finding a resolution of the 1973 takeover of Wounded Knee the Pine Ridge Indian Reservation in South Dakota. For his work as a mediator on this dispute, he was given a citation by President Richard Nixon. In 1978, he played a key role in resolving a dispute involving whether American Nazis could hold a march in Skokie, Illinois, which had a predominately Jewish population. Because he came to be regarded as someone who could be trusted by both sides in racially polarized disputes, he was in involved with numerous conflicts about police — community conflicts, prison disturbances, school desegregation conflicts, and disagreements over the implementation of civil rights laws.

Over time, his work on mediating inter-group disputes led to his involvement with race and ethnic conflicts overseas. Between 1979 and 1995, Dick Salem made fifteen extended trips to South Africa, where he trained and mentored colleagues in negotiation and mediation in community conflicts. During these trips, he sometimes met with Nelson Mandela at Robin Island. Later, he served on the initial training committee of South Africa's National Peace Accord, and provided training for the Accord's regional and local peace committees.

APPENDIX 7: SUPPLEMENTAL MATERIAL FOR CONSERVATIVE CHRISTIANS

A PRAYER FOR WORLD NEIGHBORLINESS

O God, we pray for a broader vision of the needs of humanity, and a deeper compassion to fill those needs; for a planting of the seeds of concern for all humanity in our hearts; for a tapping of the wells of generosity.

May we live together as people who have been forgiven a great debt.

May we be gentle, walking softly with one another.

May we be understanding, lest we shall add to the world's sorrow or cause to flow needless tears.

May we be as anxious for the rights of others as we are for our own.

May we be as eager to forgive as we are to seek forgiveness.

May we know no barriers of creed or race or sex, that our love may be like Yours—a love that sees all people as Your children and our kin.

May we be ministers of humanity.

Amen

...As I have read and pondered numerous articles by respected leaders, particularly from the evangelical Christian world, and considered what I have heard in my own conversations, I have been struck by the depth of the disconnect within the Body of Christ. Many African Americans are feeling deep pain from these events coming on top of the old hurts of past personal experiences of racism. Many black Christians are yearning to see and hear white Christians reach out and speak out. But many

whites feel they do not know not what to do or what to say in such a polarized and politicized context, and they do not have the trusted relationships with African Americans that would enable them to learn. And, sadly, all too many whites are indifferent or even hostile. The result is often a painful, mistrust-filled silence... Our nation has a long way to go in racial understanding and racial reconciliation. And what needs to happen needs to happen first in the churches, because we know the One who can bring us together. — Rt. Rev. John A. M. Guernsey; Bishop, Diocese of the Mid-Atlantic (Anglican) What Ferguson Reveals and What We Can Do (http://www.anglicanchurch.net/?/main/p./939)

BIBLICAL TREATMENT OF ALLYSHIP

One day, when Moses had grown up, he went out to his people and looked on their burdens, and he saw an Egyptian beating a Hebrew, one of his people. He looked this way and that, and seeing no one, he struck down the Egyptian and hid him in the sand. — Exodus 2.11-12

After growing up in the household of Pharaoh, Moses awakened to the cruel suffering of the Hebrew people. He was so impassioned by the injustice he saw that he committed murder, which led to a forty-year stint in Midian. Eventually, God called out to Moses from the burning bush and directed him to appeal to Pharaoh to release the Hebrew people from bondage. Moses had already forsaken all the status and honor of his Egyptian upbringing and his courage led to the emancipation of God's chosen nation.

SESSION 2 THEME: HUMILITY

In the commencement I think it proper to apprise you that several things, connected with the present condition of the Africans, tend to bias the mind against them, and consequently incapacitate it for an impartial decision with respect to their rights.

APPENDICES

I. Their color is very different from our own. This leads many to conclude that Heaven has expressly marked them out for servitude; and when the mind once settles upon such a conclusion, it is completely fortified against the strongest arguments that reason can suggest, or the mind of man invent...

II. The Africans are deeply degraded. The hand of oppression has pressed them down from the rank of men to that of beasts; they are bought and sold, and driven from place to place like mere animal herds;—this fetters the mind, and prevents that expansion of soul which dignifies man and ornaments civilized life... Hence talents that, under other circumstances, would appear to very good advantage, are totally obscured. And, even after a people that have long been enslaved are emancipated, it will require them to pass through several generations in order to regain their original strength of mind, and give the world a fair exhibition of the powers they really possess. Under this view of our subject, it is easy to account for the apparent want of talent in our Africans; it is owing, totally owing, to the cruel hand of oppression.

— Excerpt from Letters on Slavery, compiled in 1826 (February 5, 1793–March 18, 1826) John Ripley was an American Presbyterian minister, educator, and abolitionist. Upon moving to Ripley, Ohio in 1822, he became known as one of Ohio's first and most active "conductors" on the Underground Railroad.

Therefore be it resolved, that the 44th General Assembly of the Presbyterian Church in America does recognize, confess, condemn, and repent of corporate and historical sins, including those committed during the Civil Rights era, and continuing racial sins of ourselves and our fathers such as the segregation of worshippers by race; the exclusion of persons from Church membership on the basis of race; the exclusion of churches, or elders, from membership in the Presbyteries on the basis of race; the teaching that the Bible sanctions racial segregation and discourages inter-racial marriage; the participation in and defense of white supremacist organizations; and the failure to live out the gospel imperative that "love does no wrong to a neighbor" (Romans 13:10); and

Be it further resolved, that this General Assembly does recognize, confess, condemn and repent of past failures to love brothers and sisters from minority cultures in accordance with what the Gospel requires, as well as failures to lovingly confront our brothers and sisters concerning racial sins and personal bigotry, and failing to "learn to do good, seek justice and correct oppression" (Isaiah 1:17); and

Be it further resolved, that this General Assembly praises and recommits itself to the gospel task of racial reconciliation, diligently seeking effective courses of action to further that goal, with humility, sincerity, and zeal, for the glory of God and the furtherance of the Gospel...

— Presbyterian Church in America Resolution on Race, from June 23, 2016 (http://byfaithonline.com/wp-content/uploads/2016/06/Overture-43-clean.pdf)

BIBLICAL TREATMENT OF ALLYSHIP

You are well aware that it is against our law for a Jew to associate with a Gentile or visit him. But God has shown me that I should not call any man impure or unclean... I now realize how true it is that God does not show favoritism, but accepts men from every nation who fear him and do what is right." — Acts 10:28, 34

Earlier in Acts Chapter 10, Peter has a dream in which unclean animals are lowered before him on a sheet. God tells Peter in the dream to eat the animals, and his adamant response was "Surely not Lord! I have never eaten anything impure or unclean." This same exchange occurred three times, and while Peter didn't understand the meaning at first, he realized after being led by the Spirit to the home of a Roman Centurion – Cornelius – that the Gospel was open to everyone. Like Peter, all the Jews present humbly acknowledged the inclusive heart of God and "were astonished that the gift of the Holy Spirit had been poured out even on the Gentiles."

The Bible also speaks of sin in terms of the way we organize structures—whether that's unjust courts or the oppression of laborers in the fields (Jas. 5:4-6). Some white evangelicals dismiss the structural. They assume that if they do not harbor personal animus against those of other ethnicities then there is no "race problem." We do not take the same view (and rightly so) when it comes to abortion. That's why we rightly object to the pro-choice bumper sticker that reads, "Don't like abortion? Don't have one."

... We must bear one another's burdens (Gal. 6:2), which means that those in majority cultures listen to our brothers and sisters who are directly in harm's way. Again, those personal viewpoints and relationships do not solve the question of structures and institutions. But structures and institutions are changed only by people. And people are only awakened to act when their consciences are enlivened to the moral stakes involved. That means that we can work for justice in the public arena as we learn to love one another in the personal arena, and vice-versa. The path ahead will be difficult, but it will require the Body of Christ—the whole Body of Christ—to call one another to moral awareness and action. That starts with acknowledging that we have a problem.
— What Shootings and Racial Justice Mean for the Body of Christ July 7, 2016 https://www.russellmoore.com/2016/07/07/shootings-justice-body-of-christ/ Russell Moore is president of the Ethics & Religious Liberty Commission of the Southern Baptist Convention. The ERLC is the moral and public policy entity of the nation's largest Protestant denomination.

Racism is the opposite of what God intends for humanity. It is the rejection of the other, which is entirely contrary to the Word of God incarnate in Jesus Christ. It is a form of idolatry that elevates human-made hierarchies of value over divinely-given free grace. Through colonization and slavery, the United States of America helped to create and embrace a system of valuing and devaluing people based on skin color and ethnic identity...

...Because of our biblical understanding of who God is and what God intends for humanity, the PC(USA) must stand against, speak against, and work against racism. Antiracist effort is not optional for Christians. It is an essential aspect of Christian discipleship, without which we fail to proclaim the Good News of Jesus Christ.
— Churchwide Anti-Racism Policy, Presbyterian Church USA, June 2016

BIBLICAL TREATMENT OF ALLYSHIP

In those days when the number of disciples is increasing, the Grecian Jews among them complained against the Hebraic Jews because their widows were being overlooked in the daily distribution of food. — Acts 6:1

This conflict had a very cultural dimension because the Hebrew widows were natives of the country and the Grecian widows' "husbands had dwelt in foreign lands and were not so well known; and had fewer acquaintance and relations." (Gill's Exposition https://biblehub.com/commentaries/gill/acts/6.htm) To remedy the perceived or real inequity, the apostles appointed men to oversee the distribution.

SESSION 4 THEME: PERSISTENCE

I've often said that in my view racism is the biggest social problem we face in the world today, and I believe it still is. Not only do we have continuing problems with racism in our own country, but racism is a worldwide problem that leads to countless wars and conflicts. It also is at the root of much of the world's injustice and poverty.

APPENDICES

Governments have their part to play in solving society's ills, of course—not just racism, but other social problems as well. We need fair laws that will fight corruption and injustice, and we need wise policies that will encourage a better world.

But we also have a responsibility as believers to work for a better world. The Bible tells us to pray for our leaders, so that "we may live peaceful and quiet lives in all godliness and holiness" (1 Timothy 2:2). God told Jeremiah to "seek the peace and prosperity of the city to which I have carried you. ... Pray to the Lord for it" (Jeremiah 29:7). Are you doing this?"
— An excerpt of Billy Graham's answer to the question, "What do you think is the greatest social problem in the world today?" asked in an interview in February 2006. (https://billygraham. org/answer/what-do-you-think-is-the-greatest-social-problem-in-the-world-today/)

...WHEREAS, Our government authorities have a God-entrusted duty to guard and defend the constitutional rights of all citizens (Romans 13:1–7); now, therefore, be it

RESOLVED, That the messengers to the Southern Baptist Convention meeting in Baltimore, Maryland, June 10–11, 2014, lament and repudiate this nation's long history of racial segregation as well as the complicity of Southern Baptists who resisted or opposed the dismantling of the evil of racial hierarchy in our churches or society; and be it further

RESOLVED, That we reaffirm the historic action in 1965 of the Southern Baptist Convention to call for "peaceful compliance with laws assuring equal rights for all," along with the courageous efforts of many known and unknown Baptist ministers and laypersons to advance the cause of racial justice in the face of opposition; and be it further

RESOLVED, That we call on all Gospel-affirming people to

strive for a faithful witness to the watching world that in Christ "there is neither Jew nor Gentile, there is neither slave nor free" (Galatians 3:28); and be it finally

RESOLVED, That we continue to call on all Christian men and women to pray and labor for the day when our Lord will set all things right and racial prejudice and injustice will be no more.
— Southern Baptist Convention Resolution (http://www.sbc.net/resolutions/2246/on-the-fiftieth-anniversary-of-the-civil-rights-act)

BIBLICAL TREATMENT OF ALLYSHIP

My prayer is not for them alone. I pray also for those who will believe in me through their message that all of them may be one. Father, just as you are in me and I am in you. May they also be in us so that the world may believe you have sent me. I have given them the glory that you gave me that they may be one as we are one. I in them and you in me. May they be brought to complete unity to let the world know that you sent me and have loved them even as you have loved me. — John 17.20-23

Here, Jesus prays what is commonly known as the "high-priestly prayer" just before he is arrested, betrayed, and crucified. Throughout the prayer, he expresses how determined he has been to do the will of his Father. One of Christ's deepest desires was that we would we carry the message of salvation to others and that our unity would be a striking testament to God's love. It's vital for Christians to grasp the depth of God's longing for unity and its link to the salvation of souls.

Jesus modeled this ideal throughout his life by caring for people on the margins, like women, lepers, tax collectors, and the poor. After his death and resurrection, he modeled it by having breakfast with the disciples who had forsaken him, reassuring them of his love and their fitness to carry his salvation message to the nations. Our persistence in reconciliation is central to our faith and obedience as Christians. Paul puts it this way in 2 Corinthians 5:16-20 (The Message).

APPENDICES

Because of this decision we don't evaluate people by what they have or how they look. We looked at the Messiah that way once and got it all wrong, as you know. We certainly don't look at him that way anymore. Now we look inside, and what we see is that anyone united with the Messiah gets a fresh start, is created new. The old life is gone; a new life burgeons! Look at it! All this comes from the God who settled the relationship between us and him, and then called us to settle our relationships with each other. God put the world square with himself through the Messiah, giving the world a fresh start by offering forgiveness of sins. God has given us the task of telling everyone what he is doing. We're Christ's representatives. God uses us to persuade men and women to drop their differences and enter into God's work of making things right between them. We're speaking for Christ himself now: Become friends with God; he's already a friend with you.

APPENDIX 8: SUPPLEMENTAL MATERIAL FOR PROGRESSIVE/ LIBERAL CHRISTIANS

COMMUNITY ROLE MODEL: ROBERT GRAETZ

A member of the N.A.A.C.P. and organizer of the race-relations club on his Ohio campus, in 1955 the Rev. Robert Graetz became pastor of Trinity Lutheran Church, a majority-black congregation in Montgomery, Alabama. Shocked by the extreme racial segregation in the city, Graetz quickly focussed his energies on racial justice, becoming an active leader in the Montgomery Bus Boycott of 1955-56. He participated in the boycott carpool, driving several hours each day, and he wrote to his clerical colleagues stressing the Christian underpinnings and objectives of the protest.

For his activity, he became a recurring target for the Ku Klux Klan, beginning with threats and destruction of property, and escalating from there. In August 1956, while he and his family were at Highlander Folk School for a workshop with Rosa Parks, his house was bombed. A second bombing happened a year later -- one of six bombings in Montgomery that night-- when his son David was nine days old. It broke all the windows and the door, and lifted the roof off the house.

After the 1957 bombing, Graetz returned to Ohio, becoming pastor of St. Philip Lutheran Church in Columbus. He remained active in civil rights issues, directing a street ministry in Washington, D.C., in the late 1960s.

COMMUNITY ROLE MODEL: DOROTHY DAY

Dorothy Day had two very strong influences in her life: a powerful sense of God as experienced through the Roman Catholic tradition, and a calling to social activism. With her journalism background, she and her friend Peter Maurin developed the idea of editing and publishing a paper to address the social teachings of Catholicism. They published the first issue of that paper, the Catholic Worker, in May 1933, in the midst of the Great Depression. In it they wrote about feeding the hungry and sheltering the homeless, and so desperate people began showing up at their door. To respond to the need they started a soup line and set up first apartments and then hospitality houses.

Day led the Catholic Worker Movement from its origins in the Depression through the Vietnam War era. She championed non-violent actions, and was arrested several times in protests against injustice. The Catholic Worker carried articles about racism and exploitation of minorities, calling for equality, dignity, and justice. In April 1968, Day published an article in the Catholic Worker describing the feeling of love and grief which rose up in the peace movement and the labor movement and the civil rights movement at the death of the Rev. Dr. Martin Luther King Jr.

In 1974, Boston's Paulist Center Community named her the first recipient of their Isaac Hecker Award, given to a person or group "committed to building a more just and peaceful world." Dorothy Day is a candidate for sainthood in the Roman Catholic Church.

COMMUNITY ROLE MODEL: JAMES REEB

As a Unitarian minister, James Reeb had preached that there was no vacation from the struggle for justice.

On "Bloody Sunday," March 7, 1965, Alabama state troopers attacked marchers in Selma with nightsticks and tear gas. The Rev. Dr. Martin Luther King, Jr. and his colleagues issued a call for clergy from across the country to join them in a second march. James Reeb answered that call, and joined in Tuesday's march in Selma. Afterwards he and two other colleagues went to dinner at a local café, and then began walking back towards the church. They were ambushed by four white men who beat them with fists and clubs. Reeb's skull was crushed on the left side, and a large blood clot developed. He died two days later in a Birmingham hospital. King preached his eulogy, saying, "James Reeb was murdered by the irresponsibility of every politician who has moved down the path of demagoguery, who has fed his constituents the stale bread of hatred and the spoiled meat of racism. He was murdered by the brutality of every sheriff and law enforce- ment agent who practices lawlessness in the name of law. He was murdered by the timidity of a federal government that can spend millions of dollars a day to keep troops in South Vietnam, yet cannot protect the lives of its own citizens seeking constitutional rights."

Reeb's death prompted President Lyndon B. Johnson to urge lawmakers at a joint session of Congress to enact legislation guaranteeing voting rights to all Americans, and particularly to African Americans who had been prevented from voting in the South. The Voting Rights Act passed in August 1965.

COMMUNITY ROLE MODEL: JONATHAN DANIELS

Episcopal seminarian Jonathan Daniels initially backed the bishop of Alabama, who had proclaimed that he would not welcome civil rights workers in his state. But after "Bloody Sunday" in Selma, he joined in the subsequent ministers' march, which affected him deeply, and he returned to Alabama to assist in a voter-registration project in Lowndes County. While the Freedom Organization focused on establishing voting rights, there was also an undercurrent of anger against local businesses who disrespected and overcharged their black clientel.

In August 1965, Daniels and Chicago priest Richard Morrisroe were the only two white men in a crowd of young black activists seeking to picket three businesses in Fort Deposit. They were met by an angry white crowd, arrested, and jailed. Upon their release from jail, the two men, walking with two black colleagues, were met at the local store by former sheriff deputy wielding a shotgun. Daniels pushed Ruby Sales aside, and he and Morrisroe were shot at point-blank range. Morrisroe survived, but Daniels died in Hayneville. Sales credits Daniels with saving her life. She has since founded SpiritHouse Project, an Atlanta-based organization that works for racial justice. SpiritHouse Project still offers a fellowship for college students named for Daniels.

COMMUNITY ROLE MODEL: JOAN TRUMPAUER MULHOLLAND

Joan Trumpauer Mulholland was a civil rights activist and Freedom Rider known for her courage and tenacity. She was active in hundreds of non-violent actions against racial segregation and injustice, including the Woolworth's lunch counter sit-ins, the 1961 Freedom Rides, the 1963 March on Washington, the Selma to Montgomery March, and the Meredith March Against Fear. She was the first white woman to attend the historically black Tougaloo College in Jackson, Mississippi, and joined the Delta Sigma Theta sorority there.

For her involvement with the Civil Rights movement she was disowned by her family, held in jail and in the infamous Parchman Penitentiary, and was threatened with execution by the KKK and hunted by them.

Among other honors, Mulholland is a recipient of the 2015 National Civil Rights Museum Freedom Award, the 2018 "I Am a Man" Award on the 50th Anniversary of King's assassination, and the Anti-Defamation League Annual Heroes Against Hate Award. She is now a retired English teacher, and founder of the Joan Trumpauer Mulholland Foundation. Her foundation's goal is "to educate the youth about the civil rights movement and to help teach youth how to become activists in their own communities."

COMMUNITY ROLE MODEL: WILLIAM SLOANE COFFIN

A complex and multi-faceted man who had studied classical piano, served as an infantry officer and as liaison to the French and Russian armies, and served in the CIA, the Rev. William Sloane Coffin is best known for his years as illustrious preacher and chaplain. Coffin served as University Chaplain at Yale for eighteen years, and for eleven years as Senior Minister at the Riverside Church in New York City. He was a strong and vocal opponent of racial segregation, and a leading opponent of the war in Vietnam. He believed in the power of civil disobedience to bring social and political change.

Sloan preached social justice and participated in civil rights and anti-war protests. In the 1960s he was arrested three times: while taking part in a

Freedom Ride in Montgomery, Alabama, while protesting segregation in Maryland, and at a lunch counter in St. Augustine, Florida.

Coffin's activism was firmly rooted in his faith and in his belief that ministers are called not only to be pastors, but also to be prophets. His prophetic voice and witness made him one of the most important preachers of his generation.

COMMUNITY ROLE MODEL: DOROTHY MILLER ZELLNER

Born in New York City, the child of progressive immigrant Jewish parents, Dorothy Miller Zellner was raised on stories of Jewish resistance to Nazi fascism. In 1960 she first went south to attend a workshop offered by the Congress of Racial Equality (CORE,) which taught techniques of non-violent resistance in the battle against segregation. Hearing stories there "about the heroic actions of SNCC workers," she moved to Georgia to become a staff member in the Atlanta Office of the Student Nonviolent Coordinating Committee (SNCC), where she fielded reports from activists who were enduring intimidation and violence accompanying disenfranchised African Americans attempting to vote.

In 1963, Zellner returned north to Massachusetts, where she directed the Northeast Regional Office of SNCC. She traveled throughout the northeast recruiting student volunteers for the Mississippi Freedom Summer Project of 1964. That summer she herself worked the phones in the Mississippi office, alerting authorities and families of those who had been arrested or injured.

In 1966, the SNCC sought to solidify a Black Power identity under Stokely Carmichael, asking its white staffers to work to eradicate racism separately within their own communities, rather than continue in a multiracial environment. Zellner and her husband moved to New Orleans, where they directed Project Grow (Grass Roots Organizing Work), organizing white working- class southern woodcutters, paper workers, and poultry and catfish processors, and leading them to work in coalition with black unionists. Zellner proclaimed that this ten-year project "proved beyond a shadow of a doubt that on a grass-roots level, it is possible to create working-class interracial coalitions."

APPENDICES

COMMUNITY ROLE MODEL: CLARENCE JORDAN AND THE KOINONIA FARM

Koinonia is a collective farm founded in 1942 in Sumter County, Georgia by Southern Baptists Clarence and Florence Jordan and Northern Baptists Martin and Mabel England. This interracial co-operative was aimed at alleviating the poverty of sharecropping in a Christian environment, in which a community of believers would share their lives and resources, as did the first Christian community described in Acts.

According to their website, "Koinonians emphasized the brotherhood and sisterhood of all people. When we could afford to hire seasonal help, Black and White workers were paid a fair, equal wage. When the community and its guests prayed or ate a meal, we all sat together at the table, regardless of color. Our commitment to racial equality, pacifism, and economic sharing brought bullets, bombs, and a boycott in the 1950s as the Ku Klux Klan and others attempted to force us out. We responded with prayer, nonviolent resistance, and a renewed commitment to live the Gospel. We created a mail-order business, which continues to sustain our community today."

Believing that all in need should have access to land and property, in 1968 Clarence Jordan proposed a Fund for Humanity, in which donors provided non-interest loans to build houses for poor residents of Sumter County. Five years later Koinonia couple Millard and Linda Fuller decided to take the idea of partnership housing to Zaire, where they oversaw the construction of 114 new houses before returning to the farm. Habitat for Humanity International was developed from Kononia's plan to provide improved housing to the poor.

Made in the USA
Columbia, SC
15 June 2019